Simple Money 4 You

Simple Money 4 You

An Introduction to Money Matters for All Ages

Helen Hutcheson

BALBOA
PRESS
A DIVISION OF HAY HOUSE

Copyright © 2013 Helen Hutcheson

All rights reserved. No part of this book may be used or reproduced by any means, graphic, electronic, or mechanical, including photocopying, recording, taping or by any information storage retrieval system without the written permission of the publisher except in the case of brief quotations embodied in critical articles and reviews.

Illustrated by Jane Grimmond

Balboa Press books may be ordered through booksellers or by contacting:

Balboa Press
A Division of Hay House
1663 Liberty Drive
Bloomington, IN 47403
www.balboapress.com.au
1-(877) 407-4847

ISBN: 978-1-4525-1039-2 (sc)
ISBN: 978-1-4525-1043-9 (e)

Because of the dynamic nature of the Internet, any web addresses or links contained in this book may have changed since publication and may no longer be valid. The views expressed in this work are solely those of the author and do not necessarily reflect the views of the publisher, and the publisher hereby disclaims any responsibility for them.

The information, ideas, and suggestions in this book are not intended to render professional advice. Before following any suggestions contained in this book, you should consult your personal accountant or other financial advisor. Neither the author nor the publisher shall be liable or responsible for any loss or damage allegedly arising as a consequence of your use or application of any information or suggestions in this book.

Balboa Press rev. date: 06/04/2013

To all the readers who are champions in their own right, but need a little help understanding money matters.

If this book can help you achieve financial independence and give you the confidence to deal with your money matters, I have succeeded.

Good luck and please contact me via my web pages should you have any concerns.

Helen Hutcheson
www.simplemoney4you.com.au

Contents

Introduction ix
Chapter 1   Personality and Money 1
Chapter 2   Children and Money 9
Chapter 3   Employment 23
Chapter 4   Time Management 33
Chapter 5   Money Management 39
Chapter 6   Rules 47
Chapter 7   Saving 53
Chapter 8   Spending 57
Chapter 9   Loans 69
Chapter 10 Interest 85
Chapter 11 Credit Cards 93
Chapter 12 Banks 101
Chapter 13 Record Keeping 111
Chapter 14 The Balance Sheet 123
Chapter 15 The Income and Expense Statement ... 129
Chapter 16 Budgets 137
Chapter 17 Cash flow 151
Chapter 18 Tax 157
Chapter 19 Review 171
Chapter 20 Insurance 177

Chapter 21 Filing 183

Chapter 22 Business 189

Chapter 23 Fringe Benefits 195

Chapter 24 Holidays 199

Chapter 25 Investing 207

Chapter 26 Retirement 225

Chapter 27 Superannuation 237

Chapter 28 World Economy 245

Conclusion 253

Helpful Websites 255

Sample Worksheets 257

Introduction

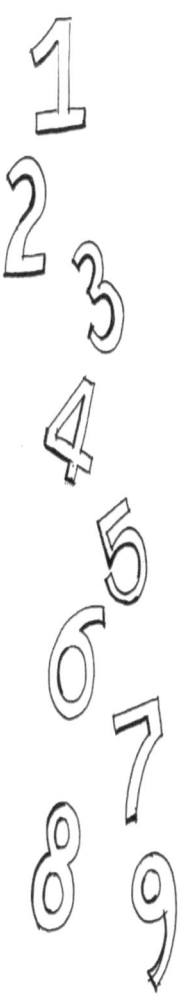

Throughout life, we all make many decisions about money. Almost every decision you make has a monetary impact—whether it is a simple decision to buy a cake for morning tea or not, to buy a house or rent, or where to invest or save your money.

Money Talks

Decisions are made depending on the information you have and how you assess the benefits, disadvantages, penalties, and risks. This book is full of information designed to help you make the best decisions.

Make Money Work for You

Learning about money is like learning a new language. People find this difficult because they get caught in the jumble of terms and rules. However, with a basic knowledge and understanding of how money systems work, most readers will benefit in everyday life, saving money, time, and effort.

Enjoy Learning—Seek to Understand

Introduction

This book is primarily about money; and most people have heard that:

Time is Money

The chapter on time management describes how changing your outlook on time can benefit you and save money in the process.

The book has been divided into small chapters to allow the reader to investigate the areas that are of current interest. There is no need to read the book from cover to cover; simply turn to the chapter you need information about. At different times, you will need information from different sections, so keep the book handy.

Each chapter heading is a single word with a simple definition. They include examples to help you grasp the topics. Worksheets can be found at the back of the book and Excel worksheets, can be accessed on the website. I hope you enjoy this book and pass it on to others so more people can find their way through the maze of numbers.

Chapter 1

Personality and Money

Your Personality Influences Your Priorities, Your Risk Level and Your Decision-Making Skills

What Type of Person Are You?

Most people favour numbers or words. Which type are you?

Numbers-based people (left-brain thinkers) are linear thinkers. They are, logical, mathematical, and able to make quick decisions. Things are right or wrong, black or white. They don't understand an illogical person's viewpoint.

Word-based people (right-brain thinkers) tend to be more creative, intuitive, and conceptual. They like designing things and can appear illogical to their numerical friends. They often ponder over a decision, weighing up all the pros and cons and can sway between decisions.

Of course, many of us are a little bit of both, but we all favour one side or the other. Understanding what type of person you are can help you make better decisions about money. This also applies to people you associate with. Working with people of the opposite type can help you make balanced decisions. If you need more time to make a decision, don't be pushed around by an impatient numbers person!

Decision Making

Decision making is all about information. If you have the right information at the right time, you can make the right decision for *you*. However, many people have trouble making decisions.

- Do you watch things happen?
- Do you make things happen?
- Do you wonder what happened?

Which One Are You?

Chapter 1

Which One Do You Want To Be?

To improve your decision-making skills, consider:

Knowledge

The more familiar you are with how something works, the better equipped you will be to make a decision. Knowledge is power. Research is critical for any big decision.

Practice Making Decisions

Making a decision is better than sitting on the fence. Practice making decisions—even if they are not spoken—to gain the confidence to make more important decisions.

Don't Be Scared

We all make good and bad decisions so don't worry if you have made a bad decision. Try to learn from the mistake and do not repeat it the next time.

> Consider a poor meal choice at a restaurant. It is not the end of the world, but you probably won't order that same meal again at the same restaurant. Your information on the menu has grown. Next time, you can make a better decision.

You can reverse many bad decisions.

Learn From Previous Decisions

Review all the decisions you make in the day and identify them as good or bad. Work out why you made that decision—and how you can make a better choice next time.

Make Your Decisions

Do not choose something you do not really want. This does not mean you should not compromise, but ensure *you* are happy with *your* decision.

> "Whenever you see a successful business, someone once made a courageous decision"
> *Peter Drucker, Management Consultant*

Risks

People have different attitudes when it comes to risks. Knowing your risk factors will help you and financial advisors assess the best options for you and your money.

Examples of Risk

> ➢ How much do you spend on lottery tickets, poker machines, gambling, etc.? How much are you prepared to lose without a guaranteed win?

Chapter 1

> ➤ Do you like to save for big expenses? Do you borrow to pay for them and then repay the debt?
> ➤ How do you operate a credit card? Do you pay it off as soon as the statement comes in—or do you pay it off over many months?

Risk is generally linked to trust—which is built over time. Therefore once you trust someone—or trust the outcome will be repeated—you are prepared to do the same thing again.

> *If you put your money in the bank, it is safe to trust that the bank will give it back to you—when you want it. If you put your money in a poker machine, it most likely will not give you the money back!*

Comfort Zone

People like to live within their own comfort zones; although they may visit other zones, they will not stay there for very long.

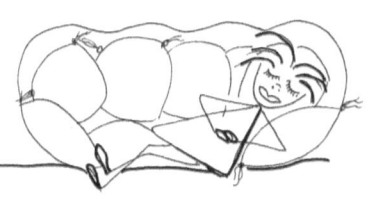

Consider your comfort zone in terms of a cosy bed. If it gets too hot, you will not be able to sleep at night. You will be tossing and turning to find a cooler spot. If it gets too cold, you will be curling up and restricting your movement.

Personality and Money

If you dabble in risky areas—where the going is heated—you will toss and turn over the decisions you are making. You will not sleep well at night; however, if you do nothing and let the status quo remain, you will find yourself restricted and unable to sleep. Choose the right temperature for your personality and understand that everyone is different.

Correct Risk Level = Sleeping Well at Night.

Example: Investment

> *Cash in the bank, particularly in Australia, is very solid, however sometimes it may only just keep up with inflation. You are not really producing any extra money at all. This is careful but restrictive investing.*

Using the simple test of hot and cold, we can group common investments into risk areas as follows:

Casino winnings	very hot
Speculative (unproven) share trading	hot
Blue chip (proven) share ownership	warm
Property ownership	cool
Cash in the bank	cold

> *Buying and selling shares in companies that do not have a financial track record can produce fantastic profits; however, it also carries a high degree of risk.*

Chapter 1

When dealing with money decisions, *you* must be happy with *your* decision—and *you* must be able to sleep at night. No matter what anyone else say.

You Need to Be Comfortable with Your Decision.

Money is the major cause of stress in many relationships. It can be aggravated because one person sleeps in a hot bed—and the other sleeps in a cold bed. Understanding money management gives you the power and confidence to make financial decisions that you will be happy and comfortable with. It will also help you communicate your decisions with the people around you so they support rather than oppose the decisions.

Help

- Some people seek advice from professionals, books, friends, businesses, banks, accountants, or financial advisers.
- Some people research and work things out themselves. The Internet can assist greatly; however, this process can be slow—and you may draw wrong conclusions.
- Some people don't do anything. They just wait to see what everyone else does—and they copy them.

Timeline of Life

As we go through life, our wants, needs, family requirements, and goals change. The timeline of life is all about the changes that are going on in your life. Many people do not succeed in balancing their goals with the changing times—and having the money to support them.

Why do our goals change?
- Health Status
- Wealth Status
- What you own (Assets)
- Knowledge
- Family Life

If your health is good, the next major hurdle is usually money. Good money decisions at the right times make future decisions easier. When the time comes to change:
- Obtain accurate information.
- Consider the impact on your future.
- Assess your risk factors.
- Make a clear decision rather than sitting on the fence.

Today Is the Start of the Rest of Your Life.

Try to understand and accept change as a means to a better future—and do not be afraid of doing things differently. Change is all around us. Enjoy a new beginning every day. Accept that you have the ability to produce a new ending.

What Will Your Ending Be?

Chapter 2

Children and Money

Teaching Children about Money

As children strive to be independent, they need to understand and manage their money in order to help them achieve their goals.

Talk to your children about money, its value, what it can buy, and how to save it. Explain and demonstrate how you use money, (cash, cheques, credit cards, and electronic banking). Discuss how to shop, borrow, and lend money. Show them what a bank statement and a loan document look like. Children who watch their parents will repeat what they learn.

Children do not need real money because their parents are in charge of buying meals, birthday presents, keeping them dressed and interested with toys, sending them to school and taking them on holidays. As they grow older, these things become their responsibilities. How they handle money will depend on what they learned as children.

Below are some general guidelines for teaching children about money. Children are different, and families are unique. Customize the amounts and rewards in this guide to suit your family. Remember to ask the children for suggestions too.

First Steps

Children under the age of 3 do not need to know about money—except that it is not a toy. Do not let them play with real money. If they understand your wallet and your money are important to you, they will value it in the future.

Starting School

Once children start school, they are exposed to a wide range of other children. They see firsthand what they have and don't have. They also start wanting things of their own.

"I want . . . ." may become a child's favourite saying.

Rather than saying "no" to your child, teach them about money, savings, goals and consequences.
Once they understand how useful money can be, they will learn quickly and soon have bargaining down to a fine art!

> *Simple lessons:*
> - *Do something for someone else = **earn** money*
> - *Want something special = **save** up for it*
> - *Save enough money and **buy** something special = **Goal***

During early school years (when children are between 5 and 10), parents can start teaching them about money by simply handling the various coins and notes. They will learn how to count at school. These skills can be practiced with real money—adding and subtracting money at shops shows saving and spending. Children can learn how to find out the price of goods, how to pay for goods at the checkout and how to check any change they receive. At this point, for simplicity, it is best to deal in cash only. Lessons must be simple, real and easy to understand. They can be presented as a game to encourage children to participate. Explain the relationship between going to work and earning money. Some children:

> Think money grows on trees.
> Others believe there is a never-ending supply of money in Mum's wallet.

> Many think parents can just go the ATM to get more money.

Pocket Money

How much pocket money a child receives is not as important as *why* the child receives money. Parents need to remember that pocket money is about teaching children how to use and the value of money. It should be given as a reward. Each family can set perimeters for the rewards. Involving the children in the tasks and the rewards will help keep them interested.

Some families have jobs that need to be completed without receiving any rewards. These family jobs apply to all members of the family, including Mum and Dad. These include keeping your room clean. Extra jobs such as cleaning the kitchen can be rewarded with money.

Payment for jobs can be given as:
- ✓ An amount per job completed
- ✓ A set amount each week
- ✓ A bonus system for good effort around the house and/or at school

The system each family agrees to will depend on the individual family. It is not supposed to be a huge task to administer; keep it simple. Be prepared to adjust the system depending on the age and personality of the child.

Earning Money

What can they do with money? There are 2 choices.

Chapter 2

Spend Your Money Right Now. Or Save it for Later.

Savings should be rewarded, usually in the form of something bigger than what can be afforded today.

> *For instance, you can spend all your money on a lolly today or save each week and buy a new toy next month.*

Saving Should to be Fun.

If you use a see-through money box for saving, the child can see the money grow. This will encourage them to save more.

Show children that you support their savings plans. Help them write down their saving goals—and their plan for achieving them. Sometimes it is worth matching your child's saving—dollar for dollar—or creating extra ways they can save for a special item.

Children will learn by watching others, including siblings, parents, extended family and friends. Learning usually involves making mistakes. It is important to make money decisions and mistakes while the amounts of money are relatively small. This allows children to learn and gain experience. Be careful not to penalize your children's mistakes early in life while they learn to manage their money. Instead, clearly explain what would have been a better way to handle their money.

Mistakes can be fixed by parent intervention.
Poorly spent money can be replaced, by a parent, for a cuddle or a cup of tea.

Practice Makes Perfect

Many parents forget to stop buying their children things as they grow and become financially independent. It is important for a child to gradually take over the payments of their own expenses. Children should be encouraged to earn money, save money, and pay for goods themselves. This is fundamental to the child's understanding of the value of money decisions. If children receive money for no reason—and never need to buy anything themselves, because they ask Mum or Dad to buy it—the money they earn has no value. There will be no need for them to earn money. Earning money becomes a game; they can play it when they want and not play if they don't want to. Some children say,

"I can always get money from Mum or Dad!"
Discourage this behaviour early.

Most children are far less keen to part with money they have earned than they are to spend someone else's money.

Younger Teenagers

This is the age of independence, and understanding money is an important area of all teenagers' lives. Between the ages of 10 and 15, younger teenagers are susceptible to peer pressure. The lessons learnt in earlier years will help them through this next learning phase. At this time, it is important for the younger teenager to be held accountable for *their* money decisions. Independence comes with responsibility. The money games from earlier years need to be phased out. The value of saving should be continued as they learn to earn money and save for something special—something Mum or Dad won't buy them.

What is Something Special?

Below is a guide to parent purchases and child purchases (something special). The basic rule I have used is:

> Necessary items are parent expenses.
> Luxury items are child expenses.

Parent Purchases and Child Purchases

Food—Parents pay for regular meals and events the whole family joins in. For example, everyone receives Easter eggs at Easter. Children pay for treats, lollies, and desserts.

Clothing—Parents pay for regular clothes, school clothes, and special clothes the whole family receives. If you go on a holiday, everyone receives a new T-shirt. Children pay for special items, such as badges or caps (something only they receive).

Toys—Families will have many ideas about when and how much to spend on toys for their children. In our family, toys are usually only given for birthdays and Christmas. This gives children a large area of special items (toys) to buy, and it makes birthday and Christmas presents more special. Try to remember that toys are not necessities in life. Do not give in to your children by buying gifts all year round.

School Supplies—Parents should buy the necessary purchases for the school year. The first year at school can be quite a large expense. For second and subsequent years, review last year's supplies to see if any can be used for this year (scissors) or need to be replaced (an unused writing book). It is not always necessary to buy all new items each year, although it is a good time to refresh old items. This also encourages recycling. Children pay for the special items, such as fancy pencils.

Activities—It helps to have a general rule (2 activities per week), which can be bent if something special comes along. This will help you budget money and time. The number of activities may depend on the number of children you have. Parents with only one child have more time than a family with 4 children. Use the general rule to ascertain what items within the activity are parent costs and what are paid for by the children. Uniforms and club fees may be parent costs, but a special hat or badge is a child's cost.

<u>Helen's Tip:</u>

Do not underestimate a child's ability to earn and save. Encourage these habits; they are lifelong traits.

Older Teenagers

Older teenagers, (15 to 20 years) are able to apply for jobs, earn money from outside the family, and make decisions about more important expenses.

Parents need to step back and let older teenagers learn the money lessons slowly. Mistakes will be made—and money will be spent and wasted—but it is important that older teenagers learn from their mistakes rather than be criticized. Every person

Chapter 2

will spend money on different goods; let your older teenager make his or her own decision about what to buy and when to buy it. Encourage them to ask for your advice, but do not force your advice on them. They must make their own decisions and bear the consequences.

There are a number of classic money lessons that older teenagers will progress through;

- How can I earn money?
- How much can I earn?
- What is the value of what I earn in goods? (When I work for 4 hours, I earn enough money to buy 2 DVDs).
- How much can I save?
- How can I budget?
- Committing to repay a simple loan, for example borrowing from Mum or Dad.
- Committing to a contract—for example, a phone bill.

A *mobile phone* is one of the first acquisitions with a regular commitment to pay. Owning a phone has great benefits, and older teenagers enjoy choosing their first mobile phone.

> *What colour, which brand, how many texts can be made, what applications are available, is it like my friends, and the list goes on.*

Owning a mobile phone comes with responsibilities and older teenagers need to learn to manage them.

Children and Money

Don't Spend More Than You Earn.
(in calls, text messages, or downloads).

How much will it cost? How long will the battery last? When can I use it? *(If I use it in chemistry class, the teacher will take it away! If I use it while driving the car there are more severe penalties!)* What sort of plan do I have? What does this mean for the cost of the phone? How long am I committed to paying off the purchase price of the phone?

It is important for the older teenager to own the plan and pay the bills. This will teach them money skills and give them a necessary reference for future money transactions.

Helen's Tip:

Organize a telephone plan with free family calls and text messages.

The next step is often the purchase or operation of a *car*.

All too often parents buy the older teenager their first car—and lose a learning opportunity. A better option is to support the older teenager in finding a job. This will enable them to save,

Chapter 2

buy, own, and be responsible for the car. They can learn to drive while they save the money for a car.

> *Then there is the decision on what sort of car to buy. Do you buy an expensive car? That will mean more savings and more working, but a more reliable car. The cost to insure the car will be more, but it may cost less in repairs and running costs.*

> *Statistically older teenagers have more accidents than other people. Does this mean you should buy a less expensive car? That means saving less, working less, and owning the car sooner. The car may be unreliable however, if you are learning mechanics at school, this may be acceptable.*

What will I do if I cannot earn enough money? Can I get a loan? From whom? (Mum, Dad, a bank)? What are the costs, repayments and other responsibilities?

Once the car has been purchased, running costs of the car need to be addressed. Owning and operating a car is a great way to teach money management lessons. Many older teenagers don't know how much it costs to put fuel in a car—let alone how long it will last! Consider the benefits to the older teenager of having insurance and loan documents in their name.

Entertainment and *holiday* saving and planning can teach another of life's money lessons—*balance*. Throughout life, people earn money and have to balance the regular bills with luxury items, such as entertainment and holidays. By encouraging older teenagers to save and pay for their own entertainment and holidays, they learn to budget for the bills of a mobile phone and car—as well as the fun things in life, such as concert tickets and holidays. In a gradual learning lesson, parents pay for family entertainment and holidays, but entertainment only the teenager enjoys (concerts, CDs, or DVDs) is paid for by the teenager. Similarly, family holidays can be paid by the parents, but the teenager pays for holidays with friends.

It may seem hard for teenagers to have to pay for all these things—especially if the parents are in the position of being able to pay for them—but these valuable money lessons need to be learnt by all people at some time. Better earlier than later.

At *18,* a child legally becomes an adult and will be in a position to enter into legally binding arrangements. This is a serious step forward for teenagers and parents. The teenager has legal responsibilities and legal rights of their own. Parents should discuss this important change and understand that their child has become an adult with personal freedom. This is the time to discuss how to recognize a contract and to learn what signing agreements actually mean?

During every stage, talk openly about all available options.

University—The cost of university is high and paying to attend can be a real dilemma for many parents and students. University comes under the banner of extras since it is not a necessity in life. The responsibility of the cost should be borne by the student as they will benefit from better-paying jobs later in life.

Chapter 2

Nothing motivates anyone more than if they have paid for something themselves. When the parents pay, the student is less motivated to perform. When things get tough, the weak move out!

There are many options available to help a university student pay the costs involved with attending school:

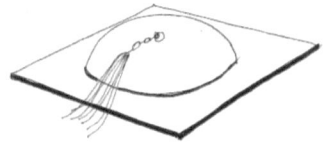

- ➢ Scholarships—high school, university, sports.
- ➢ Government grants.
- ➢ Government assistance—HECS is an interest free loan from the government to cover tuition fees. It is repaid by the student as a deduction from their pay once they find full time employment.
- ➢ Government allowances help with rent and living away from home expenses.

Parental assistance—although I encourage students to take responsibility for university costs, parents may be able to assist by providing scholarship funds or by loaning money. A scholarship fund can be set up when the child is young. Parents contribute regular amounts of money to a recognized fund or a self-managed fund. As the child grows, the fund increases; when it matures at the end of compulsory school, it can be put toward university school fees.

The growing fund can be seen as an incentive for the child to progress to university. Explaining to the teenager, while they are in high school, that you have set aside money for them for their university education may assist them in making the decision to attend university.

Lending your teenage student money is also an option (provided the responsibility of funding the university education remains with the student). (*See Chapter 9 Loans*).

It is worth remembering that many university students do not have a lot of money and are in the same boat as your teenager. They can be surprisingly creative when given the chance.

Helen's Tip:

> University is a privilege to be worked for, but it is also a wonderful lesson on how to have fun with no money.

Chapter 3

Employment

Earn Money and Keep Busy

Employment is about balance. You need money to pay the necessary bills, but you also want enough time to spend your money on things you enjoy. Often circumstances require us to work long hours, keeping us away from spending time enjoying life. The extra work provides extra cash but there is no time to spend it on things you enjoy.

On the other side of the coin, there are times when you do not have enough cash to pay all your expenses, and there are no funds left to enjoy spending. This balancing act will go on for most of your life; sometimes it just takes stepping back and looking at what you have to enjoy life. You need to learn to value and appreciate your time off (*see Chapter 4 Time Management*).

Types of Employment

Working for someone else = employee

- ➢ Full-time employment
- ➢ Part-time employment
- ➢ Casual or seasonal employment

Working in your own business

- ➢ Self employed
- ➢ Subcontractor

The word *employee* can have a different meaning under different pieces of legislation, and it must be clearly differentiated from the word *subcontractor*. Check the Australian Taxation Office (ATO) website for a clear definition of an employee and to view some examples.

Understanding the benefits of each type of employment will help you choose the best option for you. At different stages in your life you may want or need different benefits and will choose a different type of employment.

Employee Award System

All employees in Australia are governed by acts of parliament called awards. There are 3 types of award systems.

- ➢ National Employment Standards (NES) is a minimum safety net of pay and conditions for employees (introduced on 1 January 2010).
- ➢ Modern awards are industry or occupation-based standards that apply in addition to the National

Employment Standards (NES). (On 1 January 2010, modern awards were replaced by federal and state-based awards.)

- Enterprise awards describe the terms and conditions of employment in a single business and are made between employees and their employer. They are lodged with Fair Work Australia. *(Agreements lodged before 31 December 2009 will continue to operate until they are terminated or replaced.)*

A comprehensive list of awards, rates of pay, employment conditions, leave, termination, resources, industries, and complaints can be found on the Fair Work Australia website. Your employer should be able to guide you to the award you are employed under.

As an employee, you are being paid by your employer to perform a set of tasks. In return, they expect you to look after the company interests and help build a successful business. This will benefit both of you. If the business fails, you may lose your job; however, the employer will lose much more. The employee-employer relationship is mutually beneficial. Respect, honesty, and professional behaviour should be part of everyday life for both parties.

Being employed means regular work and regular income—and it should be considered a huge benefit. Without employment, people have no income. They can become bored, depressed, and restless. They can become a social burden on the rest of the population.

Employment

The benefits you receive as an employee range from legally required benefits to personal advantages. They may include:

- Regular payment for services—Money!

- Annual Leave
- Sick Leave
- Long Service Leave
- Paid Parental Leave

- Superannuation Contribution (*See Chapter 27*)
- Workers Compensation Insurance
- Job Security
- Friendship
- Positive Work Environment
- Professional Development
- Promotion Opportunities
- Fringe Benefits (*See Chapter 23*)

Some benefits can be converted into a monetary figure; however, it is difficult to do this with all benefits (friendship and promotional opportunities).

The leave benefits (annual, sick, and long service) are reserved for permanent employees and are not usually available to casual workers.

Some businesses award casual employees long service leave.

Some employers may request you take your holidays at specific times to assist with office closures or work-load variances. This should be discussed at the time you are employed.

Chapter 3

Self-Employed and Subcontractors

These 2 terms are really describing the same type of employment, which is when you are the boss. The term 'subcontractor' is often used by a company to describe a self-employed person who is working for that company on an irregular basis. A subcontractor usually calls himself self-employed.

People who operate their own businesses do not have to operate within the confines of an employer or the legal restraints of the award system. They can work when they want, pay what they want, and go on holidays when they want. However, operating your own business is not to be taken lightly. There are many legislative compliance acts that govern the operation of a business. Consider all the benefits, pitfalls, advantages, and disadvantages of owning your own business before you cease employment and go it alone (*see Chapter 22 Business*).

How to Find a Job

Most people will be employed for up to forty years and will work approximately forty hours per week. This is a huge amount of time spent working, so be sure you enjoy what you do for the greater amount of time. Realise that you may sometimes have to do things you really don't like to do. When you are not enjoying your work, it may help to think of the end goal—what the money you are earning is going to help you achieve.

Finding a job can be a challenge, but it helps to have the goalposts up before you hit the field. Is the job you are looking for?

- Just a way of earning money?
- A stepping stone in your career?
- A way to keep you busy?

Employment

- Something you have always wanted to do?
- Are you looking for full-time, part-time, or casual employment?
- How long you are expecting to stay in the job?
- How much money would you like to earn?
- How close is the job to where you live?
- What are the hours of employment?
- Will this job lead to future jobs or opportunities?
- Will family circumstances prevent you from applying for certain jobs?

Let's Go Shopping!

With a clear goal in mind, it is time to try every avenue possible to find the best job for you. Initially, it may be the first job you can find—but continue to look for employment until you are in your ideal job. It is easier to find a job once the pressure of earning money has been relieved with some form of income; therefore your first job may well be a long way from your dream job. Move jobs as opportunities arise. Never stop looking at different opportunities until you reach your ideal job.

If you love what you're doing, you never have to work a day in your life.

Where to look;

- Employment agencies.
- Newspapers or Community Papers.
- Educational Notice Boards, Teachers, Lecturers, Tutors, or Students.
- Friends and Family.
- Church or Other Social Groups.

- Locations Close to You.
- Work colleagues.
- Businesses You would like to Work for.
- Industry-Related Conferences, Meeting or Support Groups.

You can't walk before you crawl.

The First Payslip

When you have received your first payslip, it is time to decide how it is going to be used. Even if the amounts are small, it is worth dividing your pay into bills, everyday spending, and savings. Some people also donate to charity. Setting up a separate savings account for each area will help you manage your money. Do not dip into one account when the money is needed for another area.

Once you have secured a permanent full-time job, it is time to start thinking about longer-term goals and how to achieve them. The goal can be to buy something (a car, house, or furniture), or to achieve something (pay off a loan, study, or go on a holiday).

Employment

At this point you will need to consider how to budget and how to keep records. (*See Chapter 16 Budgeting and Chapter 13 Record Keeping*).

Getting Ahead in Life

Why do some people earn $15 per hour and some people earn $150 per hour?

The difference, in most cases is *"knowledge"*.

Knowledge can be learned—at school or university or it can be in the form of experiences accumulated while you work. Unfortunately, knowledge does not come quickly. One of life's more difficult lessons comes when you have finished school, found a job, are earning money, and want to move on to bigger and better things in your life—but you are held back by employers  who want more experience. This is the time for a little bit of patience. The following list will help you move forward in a reasonable time frame; however remember:

Rome wasn't built in a day!

- Look around you; *review* all the types of jobs you come into contact with.
- Keep a *list* of the jobs, positions, and tasks that you like doing—and the ones you do not like doing.
- Note the specific *job skills* required to do the tasks you would like to do in the future.

- Once you have a good picture of your ideal job, look for the best way of *achieving* the required skills and knowledge. This may be education, training courses, on-site training, or an apprenticeship.
- Look for the *employer* you would most like to work for.
- Apply for *positions* close to the position you would like—or with the employer of choice—and work your way to your ideal job.
- Be patient and persistent.

Abraham Lincoln said,
"Whatever you are—be a good one."

Chapter 4

Time Management

*Allocating Your Time to Produce the
Best Outcome in Your Life.*

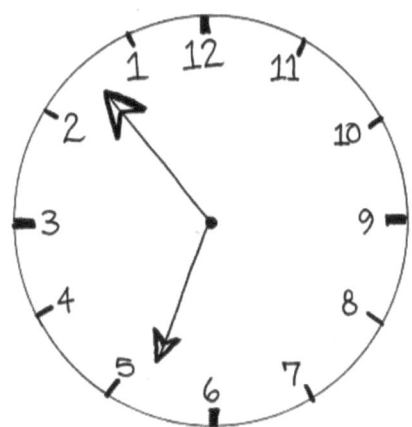

You can't stop it, you can't keep
it, and you can't catch it,
but you can learn to master it.

Time Management is used by many people; however, few really know what it means and how to make time work for them.

Time

We all know that there are 24 hours in every day and 60 minutes in every hour; however, how many people actually know what happens with all the time in their lives?

> *On a road trip my daughter asked,*
>
> *"When are we going to get there?"*
>
> *I answered,*
>
> *"At 1 o'clock"*
>
> *When we arrived at 1.05, she happily announced;*
>
> *"You owe me 5 minutes!!"*

We all laughed and thought this quite comical; however, I had actually deprived her of 5 minutes of her time. This is over dramatizing the situation, but we can apply this to everyday living.

How much time in your day, week, or year is taken from you because someone tells you a time and does not keep to it?

Can we do anything about this time that has been taken away from us?

The answer is <u>YES</u>.
The answer is *Time Management*.

Chapter 4

Management

Have you ever met someone who is able to do so much more than you are in a day, week, or year? Do you have any idea how they complete so many tasks when you struggle with the simple day-to-day living tasks? Do you ever go to bed exhausted—but think you have done nothing all day?

Management means planning, organizing, and controlling. However in order to "manage" anything—time, money, resources, or people, you must know what is happening now—and what you *really* want to achieve.

A *To Do List* shows what you want to achieve. Make a time line so you can compare it to what you have actually achieved. Try to limit the list to 5 items at a time so it does not become unmanageable.

- ➢ Write down all the things you did not achieve today.
- ➢ Plan and organise your next day.
- ➢ Congratulate yourself at the end of the day by checking off your list.
- ➢ Carry forward any left-over items.

Managing your life takes time. Some people will argue that this is not how they want to live.

> *How much managing of my life do I <u>want</u>?*
> *How much managing of my life do I <u>need</u>?*

Steps for Better Time Management

➢ Understand what you *have* to do and what you *want* to do.
➢ Plan how to get the most from your day.
➢ Organize different events to fit best into your day.
➢ Tick things off as they are done.
➢ Evaluate your processes and look for ways to improve tomorrow.

> Could I have done things differently?
> Where in the day is there more time?
> How can I use my time more efficiently?

Helen's Tips to saving time:

- ✓ Do something during your lunch break.
- ✓ Clean as you go—instead of a big clean up on a day off.
- ✓ Ask for help from others in the house—either regularly or as a one off event.
- ✓ Watch less TV and read a book or visit a friend.
- ✓ Go to bed later. Get up earlier.
- ✓ Combine 2 activities—eat dinner and visit a friend or pick groceries up on your way home from work.
- ✓ Take light reading with you in case you are unexpectedly held up at a meeting or on the train.
- ✓ Make a list and shop once a week.
- ✓ Use a *To-do list* and tick the items off as they are completed.
- ✓ Don't put off things that can be done now.
- ✓ Be reasonable with how much time it takes to complete a job.
- ✓ Work less!

Chapter 4

Finally be kind to yourself. Allow time for the little things in life: reading, smelling the roses, going for a walk, having a bath, or meeting with friends.

<u>Helen's Tip:</u>

In life, happiness is all about balance.

Chapter 5

Money Management

Make Your Money Work for You

Many people have at least one credit card. Most people buy a car—and many will buy a house. The way you handle these monetary decisions *will* make a difference in your financial future.

Do you care?
Do you want to make effective money decisions?

Money matters can be overwhelming; however with a little time to understand the system, you can make money work for you instead of being its slave.

Getting Started

- Decide you want control of your money and stop leaving what happens with it to chance.
- Work out where your money is going—(*see Chapter 15 The Income and Expense Statement*).
- Learn smart spending habits.

Money Management

- Learn simple savings tips.
- Record important information correctly.
- Deal with the paperwork.

Enjoy your money management by learning and understanding how to make it work for you.

There are only 2 things that occur with money:
1. Money comes *in* from different sources.
2. Money goes *out* to different places.

Categorizing where your money comes *in* from—and where your money goes *out* to—is the start to producing an *Income and Expenditure Statement* and understanding *your* money.

> Think of your earnings as a chocolate cake. On pay day you are given one entire iced chocolate cake. What are you going to do with it?
> - Eat it all now!
> - Eat some now—and leave some for later.
> - Share your cake around.
> - Don't touch it now. Save it all for later.

The decision is your choice, but once it is all gone, there is nothing you can do to get it back (besides make another one). Your income is like this—you work and earn money (your cake). You can choose how and when you spend (or eat) your money, but you can't keep your cake and eat it at the same time! Every time you spend (or eat) some of your pay, the balance gets smaller. When it is all gone, you need to work to earn more money (make another cake).

You cannot eat your cake twice.
You cannot spend your money twice.

Good Money Management Tips:

- ✓ Know you spending in relation to your earnings.

> *If you are currently paid $20 per hour, a coat that costs $50 will cost you 2.5 hours of work.*

- ✓ Think about what else you could spend your money on.
- ✓ Make a choice to spend the money.
- ✓ Stick to your budget.
- ✓ Go to cash—no more credit cards.
- ✓ Shop with a list—for groceries, Christmas presents, cards, and school supplies.
- ✓ Shop around for the best price and value.
- ✓ Make savings a habit—even $10 per week will add up over time.
- ✓ Keep a record of what you are earning and where you are spending your money.

Money Management

You make money decisions every day—many without thinking about it. Stop and decide where you want to spend your money.

Can you afford to make this decision?

Spending without thought leads to money mismanagement —and unnecessary costs.

- *Getting in the car to drive to the shops—can you afford the petrol?*
- *Picking up the phone to call a friend—can you afford the phone call?*
- *Reading the paper—can you afford to buy the paper? Can you afford to have it delivered?*
- *Putting the clothes in the dryer instead of on the line—can you afford the electricity?*

Paying Bills

Helen's Rules:

- Pay on time.
- Pay the bill with the higher interest rate first.
- Make paying bills easy.
- Minimize how many bills you pay (where possible).
- Write down everything you spend—you will be shocked.

Chapter 5

Pay on Time

Every bill has a date that it needs to be paid by. Your supermarket bill needs to be paid before you leave, the phone bill has a due date on the statement, and the mortgage payment is due on the same day each month.

Paying bills on time builds positive relationships. Some places will offer discounts for on-time or early payment. Take advantage of these wherever possible to avoid unnecessary fees and interest. Many people are unaware of the fees and charges associated with not paying bills. This can come as a shock—just because you are a few days late.

Pay the Bill with the Highest Interest Rate First

Loans, credit cards, and other debts have different interest rates. Most credit cards have a higher interest rate than a home mortgage. Some store credit cards offer no interest for an introductory period. Some bills have other penalties. Try to repay the debt with the highest interest rate first, unless it becomes necessary to pay another bill first.

> *If you don't pay your electricity bill they will cut off the electricity. If you don't pay your car registration they will reduce the term of the registration.*

Money Management

Make Paying Bills Easy

Deal with bills once a week—and leave all other times bill free. The ideal time is when you have just received your pay or income. Keep all bills and money paperwork in one place. Do not leave them around the house to get lost.

<u>Helen's Tip:</u>

Keep an empty tissue box in the car for loose receipts.

Step 1—When you open the mail, review the bill for accuracy. If you do not agree, follow up with the supplier immediately. (It may take time for the matter to be resolved, and this may go past the due date of payment.)

Step 2—Look at the date the bill is due. If it is due within a week, pay it now. If it is not due within a week, highlight the due date and review it next week.

Step 3—Make sure you have the funds to pay the bill (dishonouring any bill is costly). If you do not have the funds, you may need to shuffle money between accounts, wait a couple of days until your pay is deposited, or source alternative funds. (*See Chapter 9 Loans*).

Step 4—Record the expense—*see Record Keeping below.*

Step 5—File all paid bills and leave all unpaid bills for next week. Filing ensures a clean work space and finalizes the account. It also removes the likelihood of paying a bill twice.

Minimize Bill Payments (Where Possible)

- If you can reduce a bill by reducing usage on that service, it will be easier to afford. With the phone bill, making fewer calls will cost you less money. Review your plan and ensure it is suitable for the calls you actually make.
- If you use property managers or business managers, ask them to pay the related bills for you and deduct them from rent. This will mean fewer bills for you to pay.
- In direct debit systems the supplier takes the funds from your credit card or bank account directly. This can save time and it eliminates the possibility of running late. Be sure to check the statements when they arrive so you know how much money is coming out of the account and on what date. Make sure the funds are available in your account on this day. This is an excellent way to operate a credit card; it ensures you take advantage of maximum interest-free days without ever being late. *Remember that credit cards often charge the highest interest rate of all loans.*
- Combine accounts into one statement (mobile and house phone bills).

Record Keeping

After you have paid your bills—but before you file them—is the best time to record your spending since you have all the information in front of you *(see Chapter 13 Record Keeping).*

Have the systems in place to ensure this regular job does not become a tedious one.

Once you have taken care of the regular work, money management moves onto setting goals and planning how to use your money efficiently.

Chapter 6

Rules

"Commerce is a game of skill which many people play, but which few play well"
—Ralph Waldo Emerson

Helen's Tip:

Learn the Rules and Play by Them.

Money management is like any game, you need to learn the rules and then play by them. If you play well you will be rewarded. However if you play poorly or break the rules, there is a penalty.

Just as football is the love of some people, and motor sport is the love of others, each person is different. People enjoy each game differently. Although you can be guided by a friend or family member, always do your own assessment to ensure that you are playing the right game for you—and you will be more satisfied with the outcome.

Rules

Would you enjoy going to a football match without knowing the rules? What if you didn't know how each team was going to try to win? What if you didn't know the penalties for breaking the rules—or how long the game lasts?

Would you enjoy the match more if you knew the rules?

When you deal with money, the people who are financially successful learn the rules and play by them. They make the best of the current situation and try not to get penalised.

The Rules:

- Competition or Options
- Guidelines
- Costs—Setup and Ongoing
- Advantages
- Disadvantages
- Terms

Rule Examples:

Shares

Some people like to buy and *sell* shares. Some people like to buy and *own* shares. Others do not buy or sell shares at all. In order to win in the share market, you will need to understand the rules—when to buy, when to sell, what to buy, what the costs are, and what the penalties are. If you do not understand how to play with shares it is likely you will lose interest and money and will not like this game.

Chapter 6

The more you understand about the game, the more interest you have—and the more you can earn. If you understand how a company is operating and what is happening on a global basis within an industry—you will be able to make better decisions about whether to buy or sell a particular share. If you are going to buy and sell shares without this knowledge, it would be like going to a game of football, without understanding the rules of the game.

Credit Cards

Credit cards have the following rules; (*more details in chapter 11.*)

- Pay on time or pay interest.
- Stay within the card limit or pay the penalty.
- They charge annual fees, late-payment fees, and interest on cash withdrawals.
- Not all cards are accepted by all shops.
- Some cards offer reward systems.

Understanding these rules and using them to *your* advantage for the lowest cost will save money. If you play by the rules, you will have access to credit all the time. If pay on time, you incur no interest—and may have a usable rewards program.

> *The credit card choice will not be the same for each person since everyone has different needs and plays the game differently. Different reward systems will suit different people.*

Telephones

There are many telephone plans on the market today. To assess which one is going to suit your needs best, follow these 6 rules. Remember that each person is different and has different needs. What suits you may be quite different from what suits your mum!

1. <u>Competition</u>—look at the different companies offering mobile phone plans.
2. What are the <u>guidelines</u>—free calls, free downloads, or free texts messages?
3. What is the <u>cost</u>—are there monthly minimums or expenses above the plan options?
4. What are the <u>advantages</u>—free phone, upgrade option, coverage, or bundling?
5. What are the <u>disadvantages</u>—are there more bills to pay?
6. Is there a fixed-<u>term</u> rate or a monthly contract?

Other money matters, you need to know the rules before signing on the bottom line are:

- Bank Loans
- Savings Accounts
- Reward Systems
- Investments
- Superannuation Funds

Run the Numbers

Some rules are not so clear. Although cost is not the only factor in your decisions, it does play a large part.

- What is the cost to me now?
- What is the ongoing cost?
- When will the costs end?

Chapter 6

Compare one option with another option by writing down all the costs associated with each decision and calculating the total cost for each option. Remember the initial costs and ongoing costs. Once you have the costs, you can slot them into the rules to help you make a better decision.

(A worksheet is available to run the numbers at the back of the book.)

To make a fair comparison, it is wise to review a minimum of 3 options. You may choose to review more than 3; however, using less may not produce a clear picture. A common outcome is 2 of the 3 options will be close—and the third is quite different. This leads you to the conclusion that option 3 may not be showing the full picture or may be too good to be true. It is probably better to stick with one of the other 2 options.

Many money decisions are made without being aware of the penalties. Always ask questions (what if . . .). You do not need to know the rules to every game—only the rules to the money game you want to play.

The easiest way to find out the cost of any decision is to;

"Run the Numbers".

Common Traps People Fall Into:

- Looking at only the upfront costs—and not the ongoing or running costs.
- Buying something on an interest-free or terms basis—only to find out that you have to make regular repayments.
- Being offered a new or different credit card only to find that it has more fees than your old one.
- Being offered an increase on your credit card. This is done to encourage you to increase your spending—but the fees and interest you pay the company may also increase.
- Being offered a rewards program that you don't use (frequent flyers when you rarely go away by plane).
- Two-for-one deals. Don't buy a life time supply to save money if you do not have the space to store the product. Perhaps money in the bank would save you more.
- Tax advantages that only apply to people who pay the highest marginal tax rate.
- Using historical data to sell—instead of live data.

Chapter 7

Saving

Spending Less Than You Earn

Why Save?

- ✓ Savings means money in the bank.
- ✓ Money gives you choices and options.
- ✓ Savings helps achieve bigger goals.

> When my daughter arrived home from work, she was disappointed that she had been given another shift later that day since she already had plans. Unfortunately, she needed the money and could not say no to the extra shift. Since she had no savings, there was no option but to take the late shift, earn the money, and upset her plans.

Saving

Sometimes you may need to wait longer to own something because you must save, but the prize at the end may prove to be better than the debt you incur if you borrow.

How Much Should You Save?

The more you save, the more flexibility you have. Most people do not have the option to save all their earnings; therefore it is a balance between saving and spending. Some people would suggest saving 40 % of earnings; others say 10% of earnings. Balance between what you enjoy today and how you want to build your future.

Regular Savings = Regular Results

> *Saving is a real asset that will be there tomorrow, unlike money spent on food.*

More reasons to save:

- ✓ Get rich slowly! Get rich quick schemes rarely work.
- ✓ Your money will grow in the bank with interest earned.
- ✓ Creating a savings history will help when you want to borrow money.
- ✓ Having available savings allows you to take advantage of a good deal or specials rather than borrowing money.

One of the best ways to save money—is not to spend it!

How to Save

- ✓ Divide you earnings into money for today and savings for tomorrow.
- ✓ Stay on track.
- ✓ Keep records on the progress.
- ✓ Focus on the reward at the end.

One Step at a Time.

Helen's Tips for Saving Money:

- ✓ Go to the shops less.
- ✓ Buy or grow food and cook or make your own meals. (My children loved making their own pizza.)
- ✓ Be creative. Wrapping paper can be in the form of children's artwork or decorated old newspapers.
- ✓ Recycle everything—clothes, stationery, gifts, leftover meals.
- ✓ Visit your local $2 shop for cards, tissues, and books.
- ✓ Reduce the amount of branded products—food, clothes, sunglasses, shampoo, shoes, and toys.
- ✓ Save on electricity by switching off appliances.
- ✓ Buy in bulk and freeze individual proportions.
- ✓ Buy petrol on the cheapest day.
- ✓ Walk or ride a bike instead of using the car.
- ✓ Shop for your groceries on a full stomach.
- ✓ Shop without children.
- ✓ Create a list and stick to it.
- ✓ Buy quality electrical appliances. Cheap may not be cheap in the long run; many electrical items cause much stress when they break down.
- ✓ Fix quality shoes and clothing.

Saving

- ✓ Use your reward systems.
- ✓ Save on heating by closing doors and only heating rooms you use.
- ✓ Save on holidays by planning in advance. Take advantage of cheap plane tickets, off peak accommodations etc.
- ✓ Use self-catering holidays. Stay in cabins and apartments instead of hotels.
- ✓ Make use of free work benefits—uniforms, meals, and travel.
- ✓ Keep warranties for when you need them.
- ✓ Do not waste money on fines, penalties, overdue fees, or interest.

Every Little Bit Helps.

When to Stop Saving

Saving should be a way of life for everyone; however, money in the bank with no goals in mind can seem like a waste. You can enjoy saving more by setting goals. When one goal is achieved, move on to your next goal and continue your saving patterns.

When you pay off a long-term debt, (a car loan), it is a good practice to reallocate the repayment amount to another purpose. Make a conscious decision about what to do with the funds—and avoid putting them into the general pool of money to be spent.

The seeds you sow today will reap the benefits tomorrow.

Chapter 8

Spending

The Art of Reducing Ones Income

<u>Helen's Tip:</u>

It's not what you earn—but how you spend your money—that will make you rich!

Most people love to buy things; it is only what is bought that varies between age, sex, and culture.

Lots of people buy too much. Not many people don't buy enough.

Just about everyone in the Western World owns things they do not need.

How much do you own that you do not need?

Spending

What else could you spend your money on?

> *If you take a sandwich from home and use the coffee at work you could buy a new magazine with the amount of money you saved on lunch—which one do you prefer?*

Ask yourself the following questions:

- Why am I buying this item?
- Can I afford this item?
- Could I use this money for something else?
- Do I *need* it—or do I *want* it?
- Am I going to enjoy buying this item?
- Am I going to enjoy it in the future?
- Will it make me (or someone you give it to) happy?
- What is the value in work time to buy this item?
- Is that value for money?

Let's summarise the above questions.

WHY
AFFORD
NEED OR WANT
HAPPY
VALUE

Chapter 8

Ask these questions for all purchases to control your spending habits.

Don't believe me—let's go shopping.

Question 1: Why are we going shopping?

Answer: I want an outing
  I have something to buy

If you want an outing, then there is no need to spend any money—except perhaps on a coffee. Therefore you should come home with no bags, having enjoyed a lovely time at the shops.

If you have something to buy—go to the next question.

Question 2: Can you *afford* it?

Answer: No
  Yes

If the answer is no, don't buy it—*simple!* Look—but don't touch. You will return home empty handed. Try to focus on what you have achieved by not spending money. The saving has bought you closer to achieving your goal, and you should be very happy with this outcome.

If the answer is yes, go to the next question.

Question 3: Is it a *need* or a *want*?

Spending should be divided into *needs* and *wants*. Every time you pull out your wallet, ask yourself which one this is. Since

Spending

need items have to be purchased, there are no further questions. Go shopping.

If it is a want item, move to question 4.

Question 4: Will it bring *happiness*?

Answer: Yes—move to the next question.
       No

If the answer is no, don't buy it. You will regret the purchase by the time you get home. Why are you even looking at this item?

Question 5: Are you getting *value* for your money?

Answer: No
       Yes

If the answer is no, don't buy it. You will regret spending the money and will not be able to achieve your goals.

If the answer is Yes,

BUY IT and Enjoy It.

Let's look at each question in more detail.

Question 1: Why

Spending is all about focus. Before you go to the shops, be *very* clear what you *really* want to buy. If you have lots of debt or other goals, don't even go to the shops. Meet your friends in the park for walk.

Are you just buying this item because:

- It looks really nice?
- It's a bargain?
- You don't have one?
- You might need it in the future?
- What are you going to do with it when you get home?
- Is it replacing something?
- Are you going to throw out the old one?
- When are you going to use it? How often?

<u>Are you SURE?</u>

Helen's Tip:
Before you go shopping, find the item you are replacing.

Impulse buying is really only an excuse for the rich—how rich are you?

Helen's Tip:
Avoid impulse spending by not going to the shops.

Improvements—whether they are related to the home or car—are among the largest expenses items. Sometimes there is no option but to buy.

> *When the toilet needs fixing, you really need to spend money to fix it—or buy a new one.*

Spending

Consider all options before investing in expensive equipment. Try to buy the quality of equipment that you need for the job—and think ahead to other jobs where the equipment will be useful.

> *Do not buy a cheap nail gun if you need to build a house. Cheap disposable paint brushes are fine if you only want to paint one room (no one only paints one room, because people get the bug and end up painting the whole house!)*

Question 2: Afford

This question is really about what you *want* to afford—not about how much money you have in your wallet today. In today's credit card climate where everyone has many ways to pay for purchases, it can be difficult to decide whether you have the money or not—and whether you can really afford the purchase or not.

The easiest way to answer this question is to think about what you would use the money for if you did not buy the item.

> *If I decide to buy coffee only on Wednesdays and not every day of the week, I can save $25 per week. Over a year this is $1,300 which is more than enough for me to go on a holiday. Can I afford to buy coffee every day? Yes, but do I really **want** to afford coffee every day—or would I prefer to go on a holiday at Christmas?*

If you can't afford to buy the item, don't. It's that simple. Don't make the decision more complicated with more words or more discussion about the best reason to buy the item.

DON'T BUY WHAT YOU CAN'T AFFORD!

Question 3: Needs and Wants

Every person has different beliefs about what they consider *needs* and what they consider *wants*. When you are single, you do not have to consider other people; however, this changes when you find a partner. In a family, there are even more people to consider—your partner, the children, the in-laws, and the outlaws! The needs list grows and starts to outweigh the wants—and the money disappears quicker than you earn it. At this point, you must be clear about what items are needed.

Perhaps some of the need items are actually want items?

> *Look inside your fridge or pantry. How many items have been there for over a fortnight? How many items are out of date? Are you going to use everything in the fridge over the next 2 weeks? Can you see some want items that did not need to be purchased?*

When you go food shopping, you should only buy what you are going to use, before your next visit to the shops. You may buy some items because they are on special, but try to avoid having too much—or having food spoil in the fridge or cupboard.

Spending

> Food thrown out is money down the drain.
>
> You can tell a lot about a person's spending habits by what is in the fridge.

Always prepare a shopping list and buy only what is on it. If you need the item, it will be on the shopping list. All other items are wants! Can you afford the wants?

Question 4: Happiness

Memories bring happiness; money or possessions do not. Memories are made—not bought.

- How many memories do you have of shopping trips?
- How many memories do you have of holidays?
- How many memories do you have of the possessions you own?
- How many memories do you have of shows you have been to?

Do you go shopping as retail therapy? Do you need to spend money to enjoy this type of therapy? Quite often spending happiness is short-lived so monitor the amount of money you spend to get the shopping happiness hit.

> *Holidays are wonderful experiences and usually create many memories—let's hope they are happy ones! However, holiday debt is hard to repay once you go back to work. Try to pay for as much of the holiday as you can before you go.*

Chapter 8

> *A car is something you keep. You smile when you get into your car, turn the engine on, and hear the hum. For this type of expenditure people are happier to pay monthly amounts off the loan.*

Giving gifts does not have to relate to money. Children's smiles can often be bought for such a small amount—a lolly, a ball, or a sand castle. Giving greeting cards is necessary in some situations, but not for others—so choose and spend wisely. Cheap presents can often be made and are more appreciated.

It Is the Thought that Counts.

Question 5: Value

We all like bargains, but *value* is not about buying cheap things. If you are required to look well presented at work, your clothes need to be good quality. If you don't have a lot of money to spend on clothing, it is worth considering how much use you will get from the garment. Can the garment be used for different outfits? What is the life expectancy? What can you do with it once it is not suitable to be used for work?

> *A quality, well-maintained suit will last for many years. The look can be changed with different accessories. The style can be updated with new shirts and shoes. The suit can be used for many different occasions. It is worth spending money on a good quality suit.*

Spending

> It can be difficult to keep a jumper looking new; you may consider spending less on one and keeping it for a shorter period of time. You will feel comfortable replacing the jumper with a new one every second year.

Focus on the value of the purchase. To arrive at the value to you, compare the expense to your earnings.

> If you earn $25 per hour and it costs you $50 per month for your telephone bill—you can compare the two. One month's telephone bill will cost 2 hours of work.

You can also compare one expense to another expense.

> If you go out to dinner and it costs $52 this is about the same amount as one month's telephone bill.

Have you thought of expenses like this?

Both items are consumables, which mean they do not exist after you have used them—at the end of one month or at the end of the meal.

> Let's compare this expense to something you will keep for longer. A new pair of shoes might cost $49.

Is this a better way to spend your 2 hours of work? It will last longer than a meal, but will you enjoy it more?

Waste

Too many people buy things that are only going to sit in the cupboard or be used once and never again. This is a waste.

If you view waste as throwing your money away, your purchasing habits will change. Look in the garbage bin once in a while and add up the dollars being thrown out!

Chapter 9

Loans

How to Borrow Money

Borrowing

Borrowing is using someone else's money to pay for your purchases.

- ✓ Advantage—you can have something you want sooner than if you saved up for it.
- ➢ Disadvantage—you may pay more money because loans usually incur fees and interest, and you have to make regular payments on the loan.

Both options, if used in moderation, can help you achieve your goals within a reasonable length of time.

> Remember that all loans have to be repaid at some time.

Loans can have different names—leases, hire purchases, bank loans, or credit cards. It is only the terms that vary.

Loans

There are many times in life when you will need to find some extra cash. This is called "sourcing funds". There are 3 rules applied when sourcing funds:

1. Security over the loan
2. Your ability to repay the loan
3. The cost of the loan—interest rates, fees etc.

Helen's Tip:

Learn the rules (terms) before you sign the forms.

Security

Security is an item of value offered to the lender. If you default on the loan, the ownership of the security item may be transferred to the lender and they can sell the item to repay the loan.

The type and the value of the security are used to determine the amount of money you can borrow. They often affect the cost (interest rate) of the loan. The lender will generally only lend a percentage of the value of the security and not the full value. In this way, the bank is protected in case the security's value decreases.

> *If you want to buy a house and need to borrow the funds, the bank may only lend up to 80% of the sale price of the house. You will need to supply the balance (20%) of the funds in the form of a deposit.*

It is sometimes possible to increase your borrowing with the use of mortgage insurance (*see Chapter 20 Insurance*).

Chapter 9

The cost of borrowing is also determined by the type of security provided by the borrower. When a safe and valuable security is offered, there is less risk to the lender; therefore, the loan usually has a lower interest rate. A house is considered more secure than a car. A car is considered more secure than furniture. Therefore, the interest rates on housing loans are usually lower than the interest rates on car loans, which are usually lower than the interest rate, on credit cards, where there is no security.

Ability to Repay a Loan

Your ability to borrow money will also depend on how much money you earn—and how much is available to repay the loan. Your banking history with the lender—and whether you have repaid loans in the past—is taken into account.

Lenders calculate the amount of money they think you can use to repay loans by using a percentage of the money you earn. No one will lend you money if you cannot repay it in the future (except generous parents!) In order to establish how much you can afford to pay on a new loan, you will be asked to show how much you are currently spending on living expenses like rent, electricity, car expenses, food, etc. The lender will calculate how much you currently spend on living expenses and how much is left to pay off the loan.

Cost of Borrowing

Lending institutions borrow money from someone else in order to lend it to you. Banks use customer deposits to lend to customers who want to borrow money. Deposit customers are paid an interest rate by the bank to use their money. The bank will add an amount to cover running costs and profits and then charge the borrower a higher rate of interest.

On top of interest, there can be other types of fees, charges, and registration amounts payable on loans. Before you sign any loan documents you should have a complete list of all the *initial* and *ongoing* fees associated with it.

Initial costs are those that will need to be paid on top of or before the loan is advanced to you. Often the lender will deduct this amount from the loan advance. This means you will receive less money.

> *If you borrow $10,000 for a car and there is a loan setup fee of $250, the amount you will receive from the bank is $9,750.*

Some banks offer a package fee that covers multiple loans or multiple services, instead of individual setup fees.
Ongoing fees often come in the form of a monthly administration fee; this amount is added to the loan repayment amount.

> *If the loan repayment amount is $570 plus an administration fee of $5, the amount to be paid each month will be $575.*

Loan Schedule

Use a loan schedule *(see worksheets)* to list all the loans you have. Show the total amount borrowed, the dates the loan started and finishes, the interest rate, repayment amount and term for each loan. Start with the loan that has the highest interest rate and work down to the loan with the lowest interest rate. Work on repaying the most expensive loan first.

Your housing loan will normally fall at the bottom of the list because it has the lowest interest rate. Credit cards usually have the highest interest rate and will be at the top of the list. Repay these first. The only variance to this theory is if you have a business, investments or tax-deductable loans that are often not repaid *(see Chapter 25 Investing)*.

Helen's Tip:

Try to repay loans with the highest interest rate first.

Types of Loans

Home Loan—Mortgage

A housing mortgage is often the biggest loan a person has; therefore, it is important to manage it correctly. Your home will be the security, and the bank will register a mortgage over your home. This stops other people buying your home or borrowing against it.

Check the terms of your mortgage for the following facilities to ensure you are getting the most benefit from the loan:

- ➢ Does it have an offset account?
- ➢ Can you pay extra amounts toward your home loan?

- Is interest charged daily or monthly?
- Can you change the frequency of your loan to fortnight or weekly payments?
- Does it have a redraw facility?
- Is there an early payment fee or change clause?
- Can you change to a different type of loan without penalty?

These may result in savings—either in repayments or the term of the loan. Since a housing loan is usually over a long period of time, it is worth comparing your loan with loans offered by other institutions on an irregular basis, say every 3-5 years. The fixed home loan is no longer common place, and there are a wide range of more flexible options available in the market place. Package options and terms change in the banking industry frequently—just as trends do in other industries.

Redraw Facility

This is an extension of a home loan. As the owner repays some of the loan, the bank allows this amount to be redrawn. The redraws amount can be significant depending on the original home loan. Interest is charged at housing loan rates which are cheaper than other loans—making this option quite attractive.

Cross Mortgage

Cross mortgages occur when you have multiply houses you can offer the bank as security. The bank adds up the total value of the houses and takes a mortgage over all of them. They then allow the customer to borrow against the total value of the houses. This can often release more money than if each property is mortgaged individually, but it does lock the properties together, which can be difficult to undo if one needs to be sold.

Helen's Tip:

Remember that you have to pay everything off one day. If you choose to redraw, you need an action plan to repay it all in the future.

Car Loans

Car loans are frequently offered on new car purchases, by the car manufacturer or by a personal loan from the financial sector. Sometime a residual payment (or balloon payment) is included in a car loan. A residual is calculated as a percentage of the original loan (somewhere between 10% and 50% depending on the financing company). The repayments are then calculated without the residual amount, lowering them. The residual is due for payment in full at the end of the loan—or it can be refinanced and the term of the loan is extended.

You may be asked to take out insurance to protect the car, if it has been offered as security, in order to obtain the loan.

Car loans are considered short-term loans. If the car is offered as security the interest rate is usually lower than loans with no security. Always compare the terms of 3 or more loans before signing the documents.

Personal Loans

Personal loans are considered short-term loans, as they usually last less than 5 years.

A personal loan can be used for equipment, furniture, boats, holidays, or renovations. Often there is no security; this will affect the interest rate charged on the loan. Personal loans can be advanced to customers with good relationships with the bank (a regular saving pattern). As for all loans, the ability to make repayments will be considered before approval is granted.

Business Loans

Business loans form a large area of the banking market since businesses tend to borrow substantial amounts of money for a variety of reasons. It is a high-risk area for the bank because the success rate of any business is highly variable. Therefore they charge higher interest rates. Often security is asked for by the lender; however, it can take many forms—and it can depend on the individual's relationship with the bank and previous loan history.

> *Business loans include equipment loans and leases, stock overdrafts and long-term purchase loans.*

In order to secure a business loan, it is critical to have a business plan. Business loans are usually dealt with by a separate business banking manager, and regular ongoing financial information is required by the bank.

Furniture Loans

Finance companies—other than banks—link themselves to retail outlets in order to secure business, enabling the retailer to sell to the customer because they are able to offer finance. The money actually comes from the finance company—and not the retailer. This gives the finance company access to new customers who may continue to do business with them, after the initial loan is repaid. These loans usually offer interest-free periods, repayment-free periods, and/or no-deposit terms. Since the loan has to be repaid one day, putting off repayments or not paying a deposit may cause money problems in the future.

These types of loans are useful if you want to buy something now at a good price *and* you think you will have the money to repay the loan in a short time. For instance if you will be completing another loan in the near future, you will be able to use the repayment money for the new loan.

These are often unsecured loans; therefore, they will attract a higher interest rate if you do not adhere to the terms. The trick is to remember when the interest-free period is over and repay the loan by that date. Using a loan schedule will help manage your loans (*see Loans Worksheet at the back of the book*).

Investment Loans

Understanding investing and investment loans is covered fully in Chapter 25, however when applying for any loan, the same principles apply:

- Security
- Ability to repay
- Costs—upfront and ongoing

Investment loans can be for property, shares, or other business ventures. They can be long-term or short-term loans. It is important to review investment loans on a regular basis (closer to 2 years than 5 years).

Family Loans

Family members are often in better positions to loan money and can usually offer more flexible terms. They have a close bond to the borrower, and families trust that other family members will repay the loan in the agreed time. If this does not happen, the terms can be renegotiated more easily than with a bank. For the borrower, this often makes them the ideal lender; however caution should be taken when agreeing to loan money within the family.

The following rules should help keep family loans on friendly terms:

- Write down all the conditions of the loan and get each party to sign it. It does not need to be a formal document; just write down what you are agreeing to (who the people are, what the amount is, and how it is going to be repaid). Ensure each party understands what the words mean and then sign in agreement to the loan.
- Business is business. If you have an issue with the loan deal with it in a professional manner. It is not in the best interest of family relations to discuss a business arrangement with other members of the family.
- Keep personal information separate from other family members.
- Keep it fair. Although you may be able to offer a better loan situation, no family member should take advantage of another family member.

> *Grandma should not pay to have her grandson John's car fixed while he spends his money on a holiday. However, Grandma may loan John the money, without interest, to have the car fixed—provided that he mows her lawn each week. This is a win-win situation for both parties.*

- Stick to the agreement wherever possible. If things change, make sure to tell the other party. If necessary, change the agreement. One of the main benefits of an interfamily loan is flexibility; however, this does not mean you can take advantage of the situation.
- Say *no* if you want to; no loan should be based on coercion. If you are not happy with the arrangement, say so—*loud and clear*. In fact, say it louder than you would to anyone else; family members can appear to be deaf sometimes!

Guarantor Arrangement

It is common for a close family or friend to act as a guarantor for someone who does not have a history of lending. Note that the Guarantor is liable for the *full* amount of the loan.

Sometimes it may be more suitable for the family member to lend a deposit, rather than be a guarantor. This limits the amount they are liable for.

Debt-Reduction Strategy

Sometimes you can get into a lot of debt, and it appears there is no way out. Mail comes in, and it only seems to be bills. The whole money situation can feel overwhelming. You may have a lot of loans—or you need to change your money management.

The following strategy has been designed to reduce debt:

- Know where you are financially. Know what you own and what you owe. Show this in a Balance Sheet. (*See Chapter 14 The Balance Sheet*).
- Know your current loans (*see Loan worksheet*).
- Know you current income and expenses. Show this in an Income and Expense statement. (*See Chapter 15 The Income and Expense Statement*).
- Is there anything outside that may influence your decisions? What about a pregnancy, loss of a family member or a change in jobs?
- Review *everything*—not just one loan.

What can You Change?

Look at the above reports and ask yourself honestly what can be changed? What will be the effect of changing any one item on the overall picture?

Examples of changes:

- Rent can be changed by moving.
- Loan repayments can be renegotiated. You can extend or reduce the term. Change to a better interest rate or change to interest-only terms.
- Food expenses can be changed by limiting luxury items or expensive brands.
- Clothing and entertainment can be reduced in many cases by limiting spending to *need* items only.
- Working an extra shift can provide more money.

Chapter 9

> **Doing nothing produces the same results.
> Doing something different will produce
> different results.**

Bankruptcy occurs when people can no longer pay all their expenses with their income. Looking at the money coming in and out on a regular basis will show—sooner rather than later—any problems. Most people know they are in trouble before it is forced upon them; however, they do not know how to get out of trouble. It is not difficult if you look at your income and expenses each month—and take action if they start to get out of hand.

Evaluate all the options you can think about before deciding on the best one for the current circumstances.

> **Don't ignore a situation that needs changing.**

Act now:

- Make a decision—good or bad.
- Act on it. Don't just sit and ponder; this will only make the situation worse. Even if the decision is hard to make, it is better to make it sooner than later.

> *Think about a cancer patient who delays treatment because they are unable to make a decision.*

- Prepare a plan, a budget, a time line, and the projected outcome. How and when can you sort the problem out? (*See Chapter 16 Budgets*).

Loans

- Communicate to lenders, creditors, or anyone else affected by the current financial situation. Make sure they are aware that you have a problem and you are trying to sort things out. They may be able to offer solutions. Keeping these people up to date will ensure they continue to trust the relationship. This means family too.
- Try not to default on any payments and keep a clean financial rating.
- Know the limit on credit card and avoid overspending.
- Do not apply for more credit cards if your current one is full. Repay the debt before spending more money.

If you find yourself in a deep hole, stop digging!

Debt Consolidation

This process is often used when people have many different types of loans with different fees and interest rates. The object is to remove multiple sets of fees and reduce the interest paid to the lowest possible rate. Commonly, the housing loan is used, and a redraw facility is put into place to repay credit card and other short-term loans with high interest rates. This practice is effective; however, remember to look at the whole picture and ensure the housing loan can still be repaid in a reasonable length of time.

Chapter 9

It may be better to be short on funds for a couple of years, than be repaying a housing loan for an extra 10 years. As always, run the numbers and review each option.

Stop Juggling Debts!

Chapter 10

Interest

Interest is Paid or Received for the Use of Money

Interest has 2 common meanings:

- When a customer deposits money in the bank, they receive interest *from* the bank.
- When a customer borrows money from a bank, they pay interest *to* the bank.

Interest Rates

Interest is expressed as an annual percentage rate—7% is equal to 7 cents in every dollar or 7/100.

> Sarah deposits $1,000 and receives an interest rate of 5% per year.
>
> Over one year Sarah will receive $50 interest—5% of $1,000 (5/100 x 1,000).

Interest

> The bank uses Sarah's funds to lend to Michael, and it charges Michael an interest rate of 7% per year.
>
> Over one year Michael will pay $70 interest—7% of $1,000 (7/100 x 1,000).

The bank will make a profit of $20 on this transaction as it receives $70 from Michael and pays Sarah $50. This profit is used to run bank operations and pay dividends to its shareholders.

Remember the following things when looking at interest rates:

- The interest rate *payable* on borrowings is usually higher than the interest *received* on deposits.
- The rate can vary from day to day—and sometimes hour to hour.
- The rate varies from bank to bank.
- The rate varies from product to product (housing loans to car loans).
- The rate can be fixed or variable.
- Interest can be calculated based on the principal amount, original amount, or on the daily balance.

Money Market

Interest rates are affected by national and global influences, such as inflation, government interest rates (Reserve Bank of Australia) and the supply and demand of the Australian dollar. (*See chapter 30 Global Economy*). Interest rates change on a regular basis; always check that the interest rate you have been quoted is the rate on the signed documents.

Each bank operates under government and board rules. These rules determine what areas of the market they want to concentrate their business on and where they will offer the best interest rates. Most banks offer many services so the rates are balanced.

> *A bank operating primarily as a savings bank will offer higher interest rates to customers who deposit money into the bank, and a home loan bank will offer lower interest rates to its borrowers.*

Only research is going to locate the best interest rate for your needs. And only continued research will maintain the best interest rates. Regularly review your options; the Internet makes this a much faster process.

Product Security

The type of security offered by the customer to the bank will also influence the interest rate.

> *A house is a very secure investment and the bank usually offers the lowest interest rate in the marketplace.*

> *In the case of a motor vehicle loan, the security offered to the bank is less secure than a house because they can more easily be damaged, destroyed, or sold—often without the bank's knowledge. If the customer stops payments on the car loan, the bank may have an asset of lesser value than the value of the loan—or, in the worst case, no asset at all. For this reason, car loans usually have a higher rate of interest than housing loans.*

Interest

Businesses also need to borrow funds from banks; the security offered is often business assets or trading goods. Since this is a vulnerable area of lending for banks, the interest rate is usually higher than housing or fixed term loans.

Interest Calculation

Once you have investigated the best interest rate for your needs, review how the interest is going to be calculated.

Fixed or Variable

Fixed interest rates are the same for the full period of the loan or investment. This provides both parties the security of knowing exactly how much money they will receive or pay.

Variable interest rates change from day to day, depending on changes in the money market and bank policy decisions.

Calculating the total interest to be paid over the term of the loan or deposit is the best way to assess the difference between fixed and variable. Don't forget that variable rates change.

Principal or Daily

The principal or flat rate of interest is calculated on the original balance borrowed.

Daily calculated interest is more complicated and relies on first recording all the transactions during the day and then applying the interest rate to the balance on that day. This is done every day of the month, although the interest is only shown on statements at the end of the month.

Interest Examples:

> Interest *received* on a bank account.

When you deposit funds at the bank, you should receive interest as an incentive. Commonly, interest is calculated using variable rates and on a daily basis. Not all bank accounts pay interest (working and business accounts rarely do). Therefore, it is a good idea to check what interest rate is being earned on an account before you deposit funds.

> Interest *received* on a term deposit.

When you deposit funds for a fixed period of time, you should receive a higher interest rate because the funds do not need to be repaid until the end of the term. The interest rate will be fixed for the term of the deposit and calculated on the principal amount.

If you deposit your funds for a fixed term of 1 year, you will not have access to these funds for the full year and the bank can use them. If the funds are "on call" the bank must be in a position to repay them at any time if you want to withdraw them.

(It is usually possible to break the term of the deposit; however, a penalty will usually apply in the form of a fee or a lower interest rate.)

Interest

> Interest *paid* on a housing loan.

This is a common form of interest that customers pay to the bank for lending funds to purchase a house. Interest should be calculated daily; any extra money you can deposit onto the loan—even if it is only for a small length of time—will save you money in interest. Interest can be based on a fixed rate or a variable rate. Most banks also offer a combined option that allows you to use a fixed rate for some of the loan and a variable rate for the balance. This offers some stability and the ability to take advantage of lower interest rates with the variable section of your loan.

It is now easier to change housing loans from lender to lender if you hear of a better deal at another bank.

> Interest *paid* on a car loan.

With a car or a fixed loan, the interest rate is calculated and added to the principal amount borrowed to arrive at the total amount financed. The repayments are calculated over a fixed term by dividing the total amount financed by the term of the loan, in months.

Although the repayment amount of the loan is the same each month, it is divided into different amounts of interest and principal each month. At the beginning of the term, there will be more interest paid in each repayment and less principal loan. As the term of the loan continues, some of the principal is paid off; therefore, the interest component will be lower.

Chapter 10

Michael borrows $20,000 to buy a car. The interest rate is 9.5%. The period of the loan is 5 years.

The total amount financed will be equal to:

Principal	$20,000
Interest per year	$1,900

This is 9.5% of $20,000 (see note below).

The total interest payable is	<u>$9,500</u>

This s $1,900 times 5 years (see note below).

Total amount of the loan is (principal plus total interest payable).	<u>$29,500</u>

The repayment amount is $491.67 per month

This is the total amount of the loan divided by 60 months (5 years).

A simple calculation has been used in this example. In practice, the total interest paid will be calculated on the reducing principal amount, and it will be less than the amount shown above.

Chapter 11

Credit Cards

Makes Purchasing Easy but Are Considered a Loan When Unpaid

Credit card companies pay the supplier the money for the goods to enable the customer to purchase items without having cash on hand. The credit card company lends the customer the funds and charges fees and interest.

Credit cards are a perfect example of needing to follow the rules in order to get the most from this facility. If you understand the credit card terms and conditions, you will benefit from the ease of use and loyalty programs. However, many people do not follow the rules, get caught overspending, and end up paying much more interest than they should have paid.

Fees

Credit card companies charge fees to the owner of the credit card, such as annual charges and additional card fees. These vary between credit card companies and should be researched before obtaining any new credit card.

Credit card companies also charge fees to the accepting company—usually as a percentage rate of the actual purchase. This rate is negotiable with the bank. Look around to other banks to see if you are getting the best market rate. Some shop owners do not accept all types of credit cards due to the fees charged.

Interest

Interest rates vary substantially between different banks and lending institutions. Most offer an interest-free period on goods purchased—but not on cash advances, which are charged interest from the time the money is advanced.

<u>Helen's Tip:</u>

Take a walk around the corner to your bank to withdraw cash rather than using a cash advance on a credit card.

Credit card interest rates can be the highest of all borrowed funds because they are short-term loans and there is no security.

If you always repay the statement balance in full, a high interest rate will not affect you. If so, choose a credit card that maximizes other benefits.

Look at the terms of the credit card; the interest can often be backdated to the date of purchase if you do not pay the credit card in full by the due date.

Card Limits

This is the maximum amount you can use the credit card for purchasing and cash advances, including fees and interest. Limits exist because credit cards are unsecured loans; if the customer does not pay, there is no asset to recover funds from.

When you apply for your first credit card, you are usually offered a low limit. As time goes by—and you use and repay the balance—the credit card company will offer you a higher limit. You do not have to accept the credit card increase.

Mistakes

- *Too low a limit leads to the ownership of multiple credit cards.*
- *Too high a limit leads to overspending and accruing a large, expensive debt.*

If you have trouble overspending, limit the number of credit cards and the card limit. The best limit for a credit card is the total amount you will spend in 2 months, enabling you spending room during the second month before the balance is paid.

Credit Cards

Benefits

The major benefit of using a credit card is the ability to purchase goods without having the cash in your pocket. There is also a security benefit since credit cards can be cancelled if stolen and cash is harder to recover.

Other Credit Card Benefits are:

- ✓ Reward Points are obtained when the credit card is used and can be exchanged for other goods.
- ✓ Discounts—some institutions are able to offer a discount on affiliated business goods.
- ✓ Vouchers—can be used in other shops.

These benefits are provided to entice customers to use one company's credit card over another company.

Best Usage—Follow the Rules

- ✓ Pay the credit card off on time.
- ✓ Do not exceed the credit limit.
- ✓ Limit cash advances.
- ✓ Use the credit card as often as possible to increase your rewards.
- ✓ Redeem rewards in a timely manner.

Helen's Tip:

Have the full balance direct debited from your bank account on the due date. This gives you maximum usage and you never pay interest.

Chapter 11

- ✓ Before using a credit card, ensure you will be able to repay the amount when the statement comes in.
- ✓ Choose a card that offers you a reward system *you* will be able to use.

> *Cash in the form of vouchers are only good if you shop at the store that is offering the vouchers, and frequent flyer points are only beneficial if you want to fly.*

- ✓ If the rewards system does not work for you, choose a card with lower fees and interest rates.
- ✓ Pay all bills using your credit card to help build maximum reward points. *Some companies charge to pay bills with a credit card. The fee is usually more than the reward.*
- ✓ If you cannot repay the statement balance by the due date, reassess other sources of money, choosing the loan with the lowest interest rate. Always keep credit card borrowing to a minimal.

How Many Credit Cards?

I am often asked how many credit cards a person should have. My answer is—*only one*!

- ✓ All your bills are in one place.
- ✓ All your rewards are in one place, and they will grow quicker to the point where you can use them.
- ✓ Avoids the confusion of not knowing which one to use, how much credit is left on it, or if it will be declined.
- ✓ No one likes getting bills, and credit card bills are often the worst.

Credit Cards

- ✓ Fraud and theft are common concerns for many people. If you have one main credit card, it is easier for the bank's fraud department to keep an eye on your transactions and identify if questionable transactions appear. If you have a number of credit cards with a few transactions per month, the commonality is lost—and you will not have the protection of the bank review systems.
- ✓ If your primary card is stolen, the bank will be able to stop one card and replace it easier than if you have multiple cards.

Some people prefer to carry a second card as a backup for use on the Internet or in questionable transactions. These reasons are valid but this should mean a maximum of 2 credit cards.

Depending on your relationship, you may choose separate credit card accounts for each partner, rather than separate cards on one account. This will mean the maintenance of 2 accounts and 2 account fees; however, it may be necessary if you are in a relationship where you want to keep your expenditures private.

Business expenses are easier to manage if kept completely separate from personal expenses. For this reason, I suggest having a separate credit card for business use only.

Types of Cards

- ➤ credit cards
- ➤ debit cards
- ➤ store cards
- ➤ regular shopper cards

Credit Cards

These are effectively a loan from a financial institution. The customer uses the credit card to purchase goods and the financial institution pays the shop. The loan is then repaid by the customer—either upon receiving a statement or via regular repayments with interest applied on unpaid amounts.

Debit Cards

These cards have access to the customer's bank account. They cannot be used if there are no funds available in the bank account to which they are linked. There is no loan in place; the funds are immediately transferred from the customer's bank account to the store's bank account. There is no interest applied to debit cards; however, some banks may charge transaction fees.

Store Cards

Stores will entice you to use their credit cards or to obtain easy money with their own finance people; however, be aware of hidden or ongoing costs. Store cards provide the store with your personal details, and these can be used for many purposes. Weigh up the benefits and rewards programs of the individual store compared with your main credit card to ensure that the benefits suit your lifestyle. Ask yourself if you shop regularly enough at this store to warrant its own card, account, and billing system?

Regular Shopper Cards

Many shops now have a point card system, where purchases are added up and benefits can accrue. These types of cards are worth keeping; when used effectively, they can provide good rewards. Watch the terms and ensure you are likely to make use of the benefits.

> *If you have a coffee every morning and you like the coffee at the same shop, the offer of buy 5 and get one free would be great. However, if you are trying to save, don't really want coffee every day, the shop is a little out of the way, and it sometimes gets your coffee wrong, you would have to question whether this is the best place to hold a card.*

In fact, this is the reason the shop will try to secure the not-so-regular-customer—to keep coming back. Do not be held to one shop just because you have a card there.

Helen's Tip:

Once a month, go through your wallet and remove all old or unused paper—receipts, vouchers and credit cards.

Chapter 12

Banks

A Business That Borrows, Stores and Lends Money

Types of Services Offered by Banks

- Safely Stores Surplus Money.
- Provides Readily Available Cash.
- Lends Money for Cars, Houses, Businesses, Holidays and Furniture.
- Converts Money to Different Currencies.
- Assists in Paying Bills.
- Offers Secondary Services (Insurance).
- Provides Investment Advice and Support.

Banks

- Gives Financial Advice.
- Creates Superannuation Accounts.

Storing Money

In the very old days, people stored surplus money in the cupboard, cookie jars, or under the bed. It could easily be stolen, and there was no way to tell your money from someone else's money. Catching a thief was difficult, and stolen money was often gone for good.

Modern banks carefully store money in safe environments—and even pay interest!

Even if money is stolen from a bank, there are insurances and government guarantees (in Australia) to ensure that money is completely safe in a bank.

Available Cash

In the earlier days of banking you would deposit your money with a local bank. When you needed to retrieve the money, you had to go back to the same bank to withdraw it.

Now you can access your money from just about anywhere in the world. Many places have 24 hour access 7 days per week. You can also access your money via ATM's, shop cash advances, bank offices, or other banks across the world, in any currency—in cash, cheques or store credits. Computers and the electronic era have changed the way we view cash.

Chapter 12

Lending Money

This area of business is often viewed too lightly by customers. Customers assume the friendly bank will lend us money to buy a new car—when we get a job. They will lend us money to buy a house—once we save up a deposit. They will keep lending us money whenever we want something more, if we ask.

Is the bank taking a risk?

The bank is often viewed as the bad guy in money deals because they charge interest to lend money—and sometimes they say *NO*. But the bank is at risk of customers not paying back the money they have borrowed.

In the rare case the bank repossess the goods, *(takes back the goods provided as security)* the bank is reported as the bad guy and the customer is the victim.

> *In the retail environment, if a customer takes goods from a shop without paying they are usually locked up!*

Consider it a favour when you are successfully granted a loan—and do not dishonour the debt. The bank is your friend—not your enemy. You will need this friendship throughout your life. Look after this relationship, and you will benefit whenever you ask for a favour.

Helen's Tip:

The bank is a friend—not an enemy.

Paying Bills

In the old days, all bills were settled in cash.

Following the establishment of reputable banks, the written cheque became the most common means for people to pay bills. This involved the customer writing down a promise to the supplier for their bank to pay money from their account. Interbank transactions and settlement procedures grew to process the growing number of transactions.

Now, although cheques are still used, the bulk of the transactions are processed by computers; many occur in real time. When you pay a bill on-line, the money is immediately removed from your bank account and deposited into the receiver's bank account. This is a truly wonderful system. When you multiply the transactions by the millions of people using these systems every day, you can begin to appreciate the benefit of modern technology and the banking systems we enjoy and take for granted.

In effect the customers perform transactions that used to be done by the bank tellers, using the bank's computer systems.

Thank the bank for creating and maintaining our complex banking computer systems!

Not all countries' banking systems are as flexible and easy to use as the ones in Australia. Some countries do not use cheques; some do not make Internet banking available 24/7 and some countries do not have reputable banks, interbank transactions are not possible.

Chapter 12

Secondary Services

Some banks are expanding their services to include secondary services, including insurance, financial advice, and online share trading. Using these services can be convenient and easy; many people have regular dealings with the bank and are comfortable with their services. However, it is wise to compare the services offered by the bank with other companies who specialize in these areas.

Types of Bank Accounts

There are many different bank accounts available; and they are continually changing. Some accounts may have different names, but we can classify bank accounts into the following types:

- ➢ **Savings**—these accounts are generally used for people depositing money on a regular basis. The bank will pay a good rate of interest; however, there can be restrictions on the number of withdrawals or fees for not depositing regular amounts under specific conditions. Interest rates can change depending on the account; there are special conditions for different accounts.
- ➢ **Term Deposits**—these accounts hold a fixed amount of money for a fixed term and usually receive a higher amount of interest than normal savings accounts since the money is locked in for a fixed term.
  This term can usually be broken, but there will be a cost.
- ➢ **Children's Savings Accounts**—to encourage children to save from an early age, many banks offer special accounts for customers under the age of 18. These accounts pay interest on the balance and often have low

or no fees and charges. This is a great way to introduce children into the operations of the bank, how interest is received, how to save, and the safety of using a bank rather than storing your money in a moneybox. Explain the transactions on the bank statement to your child when it arrives.
- ➢ **Cheque or Business Accounts** generally do not pay any interest on balances. They give you a cheque-book and are regularly used for putting money in and taking money out. If you find the cheque account balance is growing, it may be a good idea to move some of the funds to a term deposit to receive interest.
- ➢ **Credit Cards**—the banks were the first business to offer a credit card facility, and they still offer good terms. *(See Chapter 11 Credit Cards).*
- ➢ **Personal Loan Accounts and Mortgage Accounts**—these accounts record the transactions for a loan, including repayments, interest and bank fees.

It is important to read the terms and conditions of all bank accounts and loan documents before entering into any agreement. Fixed terms agreements should be particularly scrutinised.

Bank Access

We live in an environment that takes access to our money for granted. There are many different ways to access your money. As with any money decision, consider the cost of each method.

- ➢ At a ***shop-front***, the cost from the bank is nil; however, your time to get to the shop front may make this option

Chapter 12

prohibitive. For this reason, many people avoid going to the bank on a regular basis.

➤ An automatic teller machine *(ATM)* is operated by your local bank or another bank. There can be a cost to use your local bank's ATM, and there will be a charge to use another bank's ATM. This will be applied by the ATM bank and/or your local bank.

> *Wherever possible, know the location of your bank's ATM's and use them for the bulk of your ATM transactions.*

➤ *Online*—at a computer. This is a very convenient method of banking since you don't have to go anywhere to complete the transactions. Often the transactions are completed immediately. The money is taken from your account and deposited into your supplier's account, ensuring the funds are available (not just deposited) into your account before the transfer takes place.

Cheques deposited into your bank account often take a few days to clear, meaning you cannot—withdraw or transfer—these funds until your bank has received the funds from the cheque drawer's account.

The secondary benefit of online banking is using computer software to create multiple transactions, which can be imported directly into the banking software. This can save considerable time for users and reduces human errors. Many businesses use these methods; however, individuals can also benefit by this service. Costs are reduced to one bulk fee rather than individual transaction fees.

- > ***Telephone Banking*** is very convenient since it is portable. Obviously, the size of the telephone can be somewhat restrictive on the transactions you can perform, and you might not always have access to your paperwork. However, it is becoming a trend for people to move money quickly and easily—anytime, anywhere. Checking account balances is also a great benefit for travellers.
- > ***Mailing*** cheques is a slower method for conducting transactions; however, due to the firm paper trail, it is considered more secure. Some people prefer this method. Some banks charge to issue a cheque-book but others attach it to an account with no interest. The only cost is the lost interest on the balance of the cheque account.
- > ***Retail Outlets*** have also become a means of banking with the ability to withdraw cash at the time of purchase, reducing the number of visits to the bank. Be aware of any bank or store fees attached with this method of withdrawal.

A Bank Is a Business Too

Banks and banking are a part of every person's life; therefore, it is important to learn how best to work with them. From an early age, we introduce children into the banking world by encouraging them to save regularly. From there, we move into borrowing funds. Some will move into business or investment banking. During the latter part of life, we tend to use banks more for saving and earning interest.

Find out the rules and regulations your bank operates under and use these rules to the best of your ability.

> *If the bank closes at 4pm and you can't get there before then—explore other alternatives. Try Internet, lunch time visits to the ATM, or find other banks operating on the weekend.*

How a Bank Operates:

- Banks collect money from customer deposits and keep it in a safe environment. They pay the customer interest for allowing them to use the funds.
- The bank lends money to borrowers so they can buy things they would otherwise not be able to afford. The bank charges borrowers' interest for the use of the money.
- There is a gap between the interest that is charged to borrowers and the interest that is paid to depositors. This is used to pay the bank's running expenses and is paid to shareholders in the form of dividends just like any other business.

> *Borrower's interest = Depositor's interest + Bank costs + Shareholders' dividends*
>
> $$7\% = 5\% + 1.5\% + 0.5\%$$

At some time in your life, you will be in a saving or investing environment and you will benefit from *high interest rates*. The

Banks

bank will need to pay a good interest rate to its depositors so they do not deposit their money elsewhere.

At some time in your life, you will be a borrower and would like *lower interest rates.*

> Some people also invest in the business of banking!

Chapter 13

Record Keeping

The Practice of Recording Money Transactions

Accounting is for everyone.

As soon as you have money, you can start to learn how to record money transactions. Understanding these records will help you make the best money decisions throughout your life. It is not difficult.

Money Comes In or Goes Out.

Accounting is Simple!

Record Keeping

How to Record Money Transactions

- Where does your money come from?
- How you receive your money?
- Where is your money spent?
- How do you spend money?

Money coming *IN* is called *In*come.

This is money you receive from a wage, salary, commission, gifts, rent, government funds, or interest from the bank.

Money going *OUT* is called Expenses.

Money going out is divided into 2 types:

- Money spent on consumable items is called expenses (electricity, telephone, car expenses).
- Money spent on something you have left at the end of the day is called an asset (car, house, furniture).

> *When you buy a car, this is recorded as an asset.*
>
> *The running costs of a car, (petrol, registration, and insurance) are recorded as expense.*

Helen's Tip:

Keep Income Higher than Expenses

Chapter 13

Make Accounting Simple!

Start with the basics and then adjust your records if and when you need to—as your understanding and knowledge grows.

Step 1—Transactions.

List income on one page and expenses on a second page.

Step 2—Monthly Summary.

Rule off and total all income and all expenses for each month.

Step 3—Yearly Totals.

Total the 12 individual monthly summaries to give you total income and total expenses for the full year.

Step 4—Use the Information.

Learning to understand the information you have will help you understand your money—it provides the knowledge to make good money decisions. It does not need to be complicated. Everyone is different and will produce slightly different information.

Make Your Money Work For You!

Step 1—Transactions

First recognise that you have received or spent money. You can do this by looking at receipts or going through your monthly bank statement. The bank statement will show all transactions. It is the best place to start, but you may need receipts to help understand the details.

Record Keeping

A spreadsheet is a great way to record all transactions. Enter them into a total column and then separate them into types of income and expenses.

Your income spreadsheet may look like this:

Date	Details	Total Amount	Salary	Interest	Other Income
10 May	Pay	$500	$500		
15 May	Allowance	$20			$20
31 May	Bank	$2		$2	

At the end of the month, total each column.

Start a new month on a new sheet.

Step 2—Monthly Summary

The above spreadsheet shows the totals for each month across the bottom of the page. In the monthly summary, the type of income is listed down the page. The total income is added up and shown below the list of all income types. The expense types are then listed, and the total is shown at the bottom of the list. The total expenses are then deducted from the total income; if the figure is positive, it is recorded as a *Surplus*. If the figure is negative, then it is a *Loss or Deficit*.

You have produced an

> *Income and Expenditure (see chapter 15)*

This report is also useful for preparing budgets.

Step 3—Year Totals

Once you have one month of totals the hard part is done. For each new month, add a new column to the spreadsheet. At the far right side, insert a yearly total column and add the different types of income and expenditure rows across. The sheet will look wide, and it may be better to display it in landscape mode instead of portrait.

Step 4—Use the Information

Accounting information is most valuable when it is compared to something else.

> *You can compare your income to someone else's income, to last year's income, or to what you would like your income to be in the future (budget income).*

You can do the same with expenses. Comparing shows changes or differences.

> *If your electricity bill in November seems higher than normal, you can go back and compare it to what was paid in the previous November.*

Using financial statements makes comparison easier. If you produce an Income and Expense Statement each month, you will be able to see where your money has been spent this month and compare it to the statement for last month or last year. You can see how money in your life is changing.

Record Keeping

Once you understand what is happening to your money, you can see if there are any areas that need changing to improve your lifestyle. You can also compare your expenses in relationship to how much you earn.

If you pay $500 in rent per week and earn $2,000 per week this is a ratio of 25%. This is calculated by dividing $500 by $2,000 to give you 0.25. You can multiply it by 100 to show it as a percentage. This means you spend 25% of your income on rent each week.

In one year's time, we can do the same calculation to see if things have changed. Are you better or worse off than before? If things are worse than before, it is time to review your situation and decide if changes are needed.

Look at the total situation. If you are spending 90% of your income on living costs, you do not have many funds left for a holiday. If your rent and electricity go up, the percentage also goes up, and then your holiday can go out the window. If the rent goes up further, your total expense will be more than your

Chapter 13

total income. Unless changes are made soon, you will go into debt. You need to act now!

Accounting Words and Jargon

Debit—is used in 2 different situations.

> To describe a positive entry in the accounting system.

> *Debtors are people who owe you money and have a debit balance in your records. A bank account with a positive balance will also show as a debit balance in **your** records.*

> To describe when a bank account is overdrawn.

Credit—this is also used in 2 different situations.

> To describe a negative entry in the accounting system.

> *Creditors are people to whom you owe money and have a credit balance in your records. A loan from the bank will show as a credit balance in **your** records.*

> Commonly used when borrowing money.

It is a common mistake for people to think I have mixed up these definitions. This is because most people understand Debits and Credits from looking at bank statements. A bank statement is presenting the balance from the *bank's* point of view, which is the opposite point of view to you, the customer.

Record Keeping

> *If you have deposited money in the bank you should describe this as a debit balance. It is an asset; the bank owes you the money. The bank is your debtor. The bank views this transaction from the opposite side and will describe it as a credit balance—this means the bank owes you the money. You are a liability to the bank. The bank statement will show this as a credit balance.*

Cash Accounting—reports transactions when the cash changes hands.

Accrual Accounting—records the transactions on the date they actually happen, which is not necessarily the date the cash changes hands.

> *For instance, when you use a credit card to pay for a new dress, there has been no cash removed from your bank account. Under accrual accounting, you will show this as an expense on the date you bought the dress; however, if you use cash accounting you will show it when you take the money from your bank account and pay the credit card.*

If you buy the dress and pay cash for it immediately, it should be shown on the date of purchase under both the cash and accrual system. The change is only applicable for transactions that are not completed with cash at the same time.

Most individuals show income and expenses based on cash accounting. Most businesses use accrual accounting. You may choose either but you should keep records on the same basis year to year.

Double-Entry Accounting—For every *debit* (plus) entry there must be an equal and corresponding *credit* (minus) entry. This means that every transaction will be recorded twice—or in 2 different accounts. This may sound strange, but every money transaction actually affects 2 accounts.

> *When you buy a new book, the money in your bank account goes down. You also record the transaction as a book expense. Two accounts change (bank and books). The bank account transaction is recorded as a credit, and the books account is recorded as a debit.*

Accountants use this rule often, but due to the development of computerised accounting systems, which perform the debits and credits automatically, most people do not see this rule in practice.

How to Choose an Accountant

If all the above seems too hard, ask for help. We don't all want to be accountants; however, we all have the responsibility to ourselves and our families to look after our money in the best way we can. Help can come in all forms—bookkeepers, banks, friends, financial advisors, work colleagues, councillors, and accountants.

It can be daunting to choose someone you can trust and feel comfortable with talking about your money. There is no easy

Record Keeping

way to find the best contacts; however there are some tips to help you on your search.

- ✓ Choose an accountant with the skills that you need. Do not go to someone who specializes in business if you are an individual.
- ✓ Know who you are looking for—set down a list of what you want your accountant or advisor to do for you.
  - ➢ Tax returns
  - ➢ Bookkeeping
  - ➢ Financial advice
  - ➢ Investment advice
- ✓ Choose an accountant in your industry.

> *If you are a dentist, an accountant who focuses on childcare may not be the best accountant for you. Remember that accountants are often like doctors—some are general purpose, but if you have a specific question, you need to go to a specialist.*

- ✓ Interview the accountant. You are paying their bills; they work for you. You need to feel you can talk to them, ask questions, and be given appropriate answers. You should feel comfortable with your accountant—not intimidated.
- ✓ Choose an accountant who speaks in your language. Accountants, like many professionals, often use jargon. Ensure you understand what they explain to you and that they use words you understand.

- ✓ Do they know the rules? Accounting and tax rules change all the time. Ensure they are up to date with current laws and accounting practices. Ask a question unique to your personal situation as a test.
- ✓ What rules are they following (*see Chapter 1 Comfort zones.)* Some advice may land you in jail.

Chapter 14

The Balance Sheet

Shows How Much You Are Worth

The balance sheet calculates your worth by listing your assets less your liabilities.

Assets are things you own.

Liabilities are people you owe money to.

Equity or *Capital* is the balance between assets and liabilities. It shows the money worth of the person or company.

Helen's Tip:
Keep the value of assets higher than the value of liabilities.

The Balance Sheet

Assets

Assets can be anything of value that can be owned. They are divided into current assets and non-current or fixed assets. The division is simple—fixed assets last longer than 12 months, and current assets change in value all the time.

Small value items like stationery, small tools, kitchenware, and clothes are not usually called assets.

Examples of Current Assets

- Bank accounts—with money in them.
- Debtors—are people who owe you money.

Examples of Non-Current or Fixed Assets:

- Property—Residential Homes or Investment Properties.
- Motor Vehicles—Cars, Trucks, Bikes, and Boats.
- Jewellery and Artwork.
- Office Furniture—Desks, Chairs, and Bookcases.
- Office Equipment—Computers, Printers, and Phones.

Liabilities

Liabilities are people or companies you owe money to. There are current liabilities and noncurrent liabilities, depending on the agreed term to repay the debt. If the debt is to be repaid within a 12 month period, it will be classified as a current liability. If the loan is to be repaid in longer than 12 months, it will be classified as a noncurrent liability.

Examples of Current Liabilities:

- Bank overdrafts
- Taxes
- Short-term loans

Examples of Noncurrent Liabilities:

- Leases being repaid over longer than a year.
- Bank loan being repaid over longer than a year.

Equity

Equity or capital represents what you are worth in money terms. It is easy to calculate—just deduct all liabilities from all assets.

This is often called the

Accounting equation

Assets - Liabilities = Equity

If equity increases from year to year, your wealth is increasing. If the equity is going down year to year, you are moving in the wrong direction.

> To Improve Wealth, Equity must
> be Increasing Year to Year.

The Balance Sheet

Balance Sheet Example:

	Balance
Current Asset	
Bank Balance	$5,000
Fixed Asset	
Furniture	$5,000
Car	$22,500
Total Assets	$32,500
Non-Current Liability	
Bank Loan for Car	$15,000
Credit card loan for furniture	$3,000
Total Liabilities	**$18,000**
Equity (asset—liabilities)	**$14,500**

Helen's Tip:
Keep Equity a Positive Number.

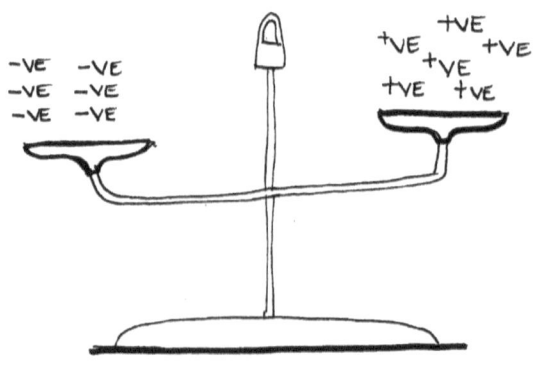

Chapter 14

How to Create a Balance Sheet

All you need to create a Balance sheet is a piece of paper and a calculator. Start with the date and value everything on this date. Now under the heading Assets, list all the things you own and estimate their value. Under the heading of Liabilities, list all the people or companies you owe money to. Total each list.

Add small items together and show as one amount under personal effects (clothes, shoes, books etc.).

Now calculate your worth—total assets minus total liabilities. Show it at the bottom of the page named Equity.

This information can be used for the following purposes:
- Applying for a loan
- Investing
- Calculating insurance needs
- Consolidating loans
- Financial advice and planning

Chapter 15

The Income and Expense Statement

"You Cannot Manage What you Cannot Measure . . . and What gets Measured gets Done."
Bill Hewlett

The Income and Expense Statement shows you where your money comes from (income) and where you money goes (expenses).

With this information, you can plan and set goals for your future income and expenses.

Most commonly, Income and Expense Statements are produced on a monthly basis and accumulate as the months go by. The last Income and Expense Statement for the year will be for 12 months. The next one will start again at month one.

Income

This is money you receive on a regular basis from wages, interest, sales, etc. Show the main or largest source of income first. Also have an item for Other Income and use it for small amounts that do not happen very often.

Expenses

Expenses are regular or consumable payments (*not assets*). The name or type of expense will vary between each person and business.

> *Examples of expenses are—bank fees, car expenses, cleaning, electricity, entertainment, food, medical expenses, rent, sundry expenses, and telephone.*

Any item that is more than 5% of your income should be listed separately; smaller expenses can go into one account called sundry expenses. Don't fall into the trap of having too many expenses in sundry expenses.

It is common to list types of expenses in alphabetical order, but some people also show the largest expenses at the top of the list.

Expenses can be divided into core or regular expenses that are not flexible (rent, fuel, and bank fees) and non-core expenses that can be more easily modified (entertainment). Non-core expenses tend to go up and down without careful monitoring.

Helen's Tip:
Keep income larger than expenses

It is important that *your* Income and Expense Statement is customised to *you*—and that *you* understand it. Use names that you use in your daily life.

> *Car expenses and motor vehicle expenses describe the same type of expense. On your report, use the name you are more familiar with.*

The more you know and like the document, the more you will use it.

Calculating the Surplus or Deficit

Once you have listed all your income and expenses, total them up—and subtract the expenses from the income.

If you have a *negative balance,* it is called a **Deficit.** You are spending more than you are earning—and this should quickly be changed in order not to go into debt.

If you have a *positive balance,* it is called a **Surplus.** You are earning more than you are spending—and you have some funds left over for savings or your goals.

The Income and Expense Statement

Helen's Tip:

Stay in control—take time to review your Income and Expense Statement each month to ensure a good night's sleep.

Making Decisions

Knowledge gives you the power to make money decisions easier.

> *A simple example is catching the bus to work instead of driving the car. You need to consider the cost of running a car and the cost of the bus fare. You should also consider your time and effort for both trips. However, if you do not know how much it costs to run your car, how can you make the best decision? If you know you spend $180 per week to run the car (fuel, registration, insurance, and repairs), and the bus will cost only $100 per week, you will be financially better off catching the bus. However, if the bus takes twice as long, you may still choose to take the car because the extra time is more valuable to you.*

Helen's Tip:

All decisions have a monetary impact.

The Income and Expense Statement can be used for the following purposes:

- ➢ Budgeting and goal setting
- ➢ Investing and financial planning
- ➢ Tax planning
- ➢ Applying for a loan

Comparisons

An Income and Expense Statement is most valuable when it is compared to something else. It can be compared to your budget, a different period, or a different person. Comparing the statement to a budget lets you know if you are on track with what you predicted would happen. This is important if you have goals planned or if you are on a tight budget.

By comparing the statement to a friend's statement, you can see if your expenses are higher or lower than average. This may help you decide where you want to spend your money in the future.

> *For instance, if one family of 5 has an annual electricity expense of $2,000 and the family next door has an annual electricity spend of $2,600 then questions may be asked about the difference.*

If you compare the statement to a different period, you can establish trends or patterns of expenses. You may compare by month, year, or season.

The Income and Expense Statement

Income and Expenditure Example:

Melissa works in a shop as an assistant. She has worked there part-time while she finished school and then full-time after school. She was living at home and then moved into a small flat. Let's look at her Income and Expense Statement over the last 3 years.

Income	Year 1	Year 2	Year 3
Wages	10,000	20,000	30,000
Interest	50	50	75
Total Income	**$10,050**	**$20,050**	**$30,075**
Expenses			
Electricity	0	500	500
Entertainment	2,000	1,200	2,200
Car costs	2,500	2,500	2,500
Other	1,250	2,560	3,060
Rent	0	5,000	5,200
Telephone	0	2,020	1,800
Total Expenses	**$5,750**	**$13,780**	**$15,260**
Surplus funds	**$4,300**	**$6,270**	**$14,815**

We can see from comparing 3 years how Melissa's life has changed. Some changes are understandable; her rent, electricity, and telephone expenses increased once she moved away from home. Some expenses are questionable, such as the increase in entertainment expenses in year 3 and telephone expenses in year 2. We can also see that Melissa's telephone bills increase dramatically when she left home. She reviewed this report and reduced the amount in year 3.

Ensure you keep Income and Expense Statements for every year and record notes to explain changes.

For instance, next to the entertainment line in year 3, a note about joining a dance club would explain the increase.

Income and Expense Spreadsheet

Because an Income and Expense Statement can be long or have a lot of numbers in it, I suggest you use a spreadsheet or accounting program. A spreadsheet is a fantastic tool that takes away all the adding up. Create a new sheet for each year. List, in date order, every income and expense you make. Detail what the item is for and then group it into account types (car expense, telephone, etc.). Show the expenses in a total column and then create a column across the page for each account type. At the end of the month, add the total column and each account column. The total of all account columns should also equal the total expenses for the month.

A second sheet can be used to show the monthly totals. This time, the account types are listed down the page, and the second column shows the monthly total. Create separate columns for each month. The last column should be called YTD (year to date) and is the total of all months.

> *An Income and Expense Statement provides you with the information to make your next financial decision.*

Does Surplus/Profit = Cash? NO

It is a common question that if there is a surplus or profit at the end of the year, why is there no money in the bank account? The reason is because the Income and Expense Statement only includes consumable items. It does not include cash you have used to buy assets or to pay off liabilities. Review your Balance Sheet at the beginning of the year and compare it to your Balance Sheet at the end of the year. Look for changes between the 2 to explain where the surplus has been spent.

A Cash flow statement includes all items (see chapter 17 Cash Flow).

Chapter 16

Budgets

A Plan to Reach Your Goal

Budgeting is about goal setting.
Turning chaos into control,
and achieving success.

Any inspirational writer will tell you that to achieve goals, they must be written down—and you must be committed to them. In order to achieve your goals, you need a plan—and you need to monitor your progress. This can be achieved with budgeting and record keeping.

> *Would you go on holidays without a ticket or a map? Would you go without knowing where you were heading or how long it was going to take to get there? Do you know what you will experience when you get there? When are you coming home? What clothes will you pack?*

Human behavioural traits can get in the way of budget success. Setting too high expectations, not being honest with yourself, making unrealistic time frames, or finding excuses for not achieving your goals.

> In the end, the only person you will fool is yourself.

People often say?

   "I blew the budget when I went shopping"

People rarely say,

   "I saved on the groceries and am now closer to my goal of buying a new piece of furniture".

Too many goals are not achieved—because people run off the rails without knowing—and then they can't get back on track.

A budget is only useful if it is being used to monitor the journey and ensure you are on track. It cannot be helpful if you stick it in a drawer and never look at it.

Setting Goals

The best goals are SMART goals:

S   Specific

This is often the hardest part because people set broad goals like travel or having more money. Specific goals are clear and simple to understand. Smart goals are specific:

- ✓ *I would like to go to Ayers Rock.*
- ✓ *I would like to drive a Red Mercedes Smart car.*

M Measurable

If it is not measurable, it will not be clear when you have achieved your goal. Using the travel example, is it achieved if you go to Sydney for a weekend? A goal is measurable if it is clear when it has been completed.

(A bucket list is a great idea.)

A Achievable

There should be a path set down to achieve the goal.

I plan to save $100 per fortnight to afford my trip.

R Realistic

I think we all have the dream of winning the lottery; however, this is not realistic for most of us. Setting unrealistic goals will result in failure.

T Time-based

When do you hope to achieve this goal? All goals need to have a specific date in the future.

Rome wasn't built in a day—but it was built!

If you do not achieve your goal in the specified time, you have the opportunity to:

Budgets

- Review the plan and see where things went wrong.
- Identify and learn from the mistakes that stopped you from reaching the goal this time.
- Try again—and don't give up.

You are not a failure if you do not reach your goal. Try, try, try again.

True achievers see it is as a challenge to take a goal that has not been successful, rework the plan, and succeed on the next or third or fourth round. We cannot predict the future, and it is not always possible to achieve your goals—particularly if outside influences get in your way. Do not put yourself down—this is only wasting time. Move onwards and upwards, find your mistake, correct it, and you will succeed.

Set goals for today, this week, this month, this year, and 5-10 years into the future. Paint a picture of where you want to be (*short-term, medium-term and long-term goals*). There is no point in saving for a house, buying a house, filling it with all the possessions you are "supposed" to own, and being in enormous debt if you really want to be sailing around the world with only the clothes on your back!

Success is reaching your goals— no matter what they are.

Chapter 16

Getting Started with a Budget

The first thing you need to prepare a budget is some information about what you currently earn and what you currently spend. The best way to find this information is to have a look at what happened last year.

An Income and Expense Statement is an excellent starting point if you have one (see *Chapter 15 The Income and Expense Statement*). If not, gather the information below.

Current Income

- Payslip (showing wage or salary).
- Rental income.
- Investment income, interest, or dividends.
- Any other income.

Current expenses

- Household—electricity, telephone, Internet, and pay TV.
- Annual—insurance, registration.
- Car—fuel, insurance, repairs, parking, and tolls.
- Personal—food, travel, entertainment, gifts, haircuts, coffee, and clothing.
- Rent or house loan repayment.
- Other loans—credit cards loans, car loans, personal loans etc.
- Children expenses—childcare, school fees, uniforms, books, stationery, and excursions.
- Medical and dental—insurance, prescriptions, and regular examinations.
- Animal expenses—regular check-ups, food, and other costs.

Preparing a Budget

What happened *last* year is the start of your budget for *next* year.

Write down the type of income or expense in the left column of a piece of paper or even better in a spreadsheet. Call the next column "Details" and write down all the information you have. Review each type of income and expense. Are there any changes you know about that will change the amounts from last year to this year?

- A pay increase?
- Rent review?
- Change of work location, which may mean more or less fuel?
- Change of insurance company?

The next column should be called "Workings" and should show how you calculate the total annual amount for each income and expense.

> *For example, if the electricity is $400 per quarter, the annual figure will be $1,200 ($400 x 3).*
>
> *If your wage is $1,300 per week the annual figure will be $67,600 ($1,300 x 26).*

Once you have an annual list of income and expenses, you can total them to show total annual income and total annual expenses. Subtract the total annual expenses from the total annual income—and you will be left with a surplus if the figure is a positive or a deficit if the figure is negative.

Chapter 16

Annual Surplus

This is great news and allows you to plan how you would like to use this amount of money. If you have a surplus of $2,000 you may choose to buy a new lounge, pay off an existing debt, or plan a weekend away. You have choices; decide what you can afford with the surplus. If the surplus is not enough to achieve your goal, review and adjust the budget until you do. Remember that you may need to adjust the time line too.

Annual Deficit

Don't worry—most of us experience this situation at one point in our lives! The most important thing to remember is to keep an open mind and not ignore this situation. The amounts need to be reviewed and changed at least until your income and expense match. Do not discount any amount as being unchangeable. Try to think of as many amounts that can be changed, even if you think the possibility is remote.

- ✓ Look at every income line and every expense line and ask yourself if any can be changed.
- ✓ Start with worst case scenario and get better—this will make you feel better even though you have made some sacrifices to get there.
- ✓ Using a spreadsheet will make the task easier to adjust numbers until you reach a position that you are comfortable with.
- ✓ If all else fails, consider a cash injection from a loan.

That's it!! The Budget is complete.

Sticking to a Budget

For most people, it is not about creating a budget—but sticking to it is the hard part. This is only training; just like training a pet, humans react well to regular reminders and praise. Once you have set your annual budget, divide it into regular amounts. This may be monthly or it may be to suit your pay system if you are paid weekly, or fortnightly.

At the end of each period look at your budget and compare it to what you spent.

- ✓ Are they the same?
- ✓ Better?
- ✓ Worse?

If they are the *same*—great news! You are on budget. Keep going to achieve your goals and you will never look back.

If they are *better*—even better news! You are exceeding your expectations and will achieve your goals sooner than expected if you continue. Do not get on top of yourself. One good month is only a starting point—keep on track before you make any major adjustments.

If you have *overspent,* don't panic. You will need to do better next month, but all is not lost because you have only gone one month into your year. There is still time to change. Look at everything you spent in the last month and find out if there is a real reason for the overspending. Did you just not budget enough? If you find out that the budget was wrong, go back to your original budget and look at the full year again.

A common mistake occurs when budgets are created at the beginning of the year, and then individual figures are changed throughout the year—without reviewing the effect on the bottom line. If you need to change the budget, copy the original budget figures first and keep them as a comparison.

Helen's Tip:

When changing a budget entry, always check the bottom line.

The "Working" column is very important. You will go back to see how you calculated the budget during the year. In my example, I have sometimes written "guess" and this is okay. If we get half way through the year and the budget is different from the actual expense, we will understand why—if the budget was only a guess. Next year, we can try to guess better or have actual figures to work with.

As you understand more about your spending, you will also become better at budgeting.

> You receive personal satisfaction,
> by achieving your goals.

Budgets

Budget Example:

Account	Last year	Details	Annual amount	Workings	Budget
Income					
Net Wages (after tax)	$1,050	week	$54,600	3% pay rise	$56,238
Interest	$102	year	$102	Guess same as last year	$102
Total Income			$54,702		$56,340
Expenses					
Bank fees	$6	per month	$78	Guess same as last year	$78
Electricity	$402	Per quarter	$1,608	4% increase	$1,672
Food	$250	Per week	$13,000	Want to save more	$11,000
Insurance	$350	Per year	$350	Expect to increase	$375
Medical Dental		No idea		guess	$500
Car costs	$80	Fuel pw		Fuel will go up Other will	
	$500	other	$4,660	stay the same	$4,920
Rent	$420	Per week	$21,840	Same as last year	$21,840
Sundry	$100	Per week	$5,200	Same as last year	$5,200
Telephone	$49	Plan per month	$599	Same as last year	$599
Total Expense			$47,335		$46,184
Surplus			$7,366		$10,155

Chapter 16

Problems

No Money

If you keep coming up with no money to achieve your goals, there are 2 things you can do:

- Earn more money
- Spend less money

It really is this simple—don't make it harder. Go back to your income and expenses and take a long hard look at each and every line.

- Can I change the amount?
- Can I live without this?

How much do you really want that new car, dress, house, or holiday? Are you prepared to give up anything to get them?

Passion in life achieves goals.

It's Never Going to Happen

You can overcome a defeatist attitude by keeping track of how you are doing. Stop looking forward at how long you have to go—and start looking back at how far you have come and what you have achieved so far.

> *What would you say if I told you to take a holiday all around the world, but you couldn't stop, take photos, buy anything, or see anything until you got to the end of the trip? That doesn't sound like much of a holiday. A trip is best enjoyed when it is punctuated by interesting stops along the way.*

Budgets

Make sure you mark the pit stops on your calendar along the way to your financial success—and celebrate each one. We celebrate when we drive a new car from the dealer, even if it has been purchased under finance, but rarely do we celebrate the final payment!

Ways to celebrate:

- Pop champagne as you pay your final car repayment.
- Mark red crosses on the calendar as you meet savings goals.
- Talk to friends and family about how close you are to getting to your goal.

Helen's Tip:

Celebrate reaching your goals. They are achievements to be recognized.

Chapter 16

It's Too Hard

This is the most common problem, but it is only an excuse. Budgets are only a guide; they are not designed to be perfect. They can be rewritten whenever you want—provided you look at the bottom line each time you change a figure to ensure you understand the end result. Put something down on paper and have a go. You will find it really is not too hard. It is just your perception.

Failure to plan is planning to fail.

Chapter 17

Cash flow

A Report Showing Cash Coming In and Cash Going out.

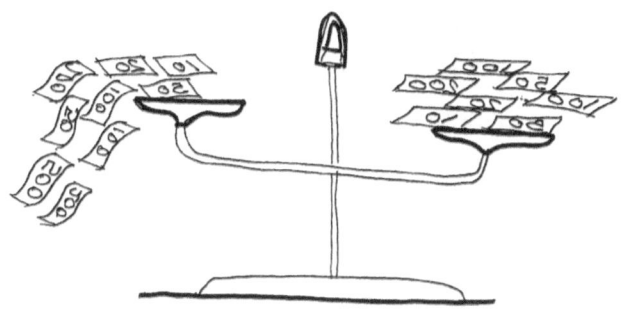

A cash flow report is different from an Income and Expenditure Statement for 2 reasons:
1. It shows all cash movements, including assets and liabilities.
2. Figures only show when the cash has been through the bank account.

We all have certain items that must be paid for at set times of the year, and it is important that these dates are not missed

Cash flow

since there can be penalties and consequences. Understanding the timing of bills and managing them to best suit your income is not as difficult as it sounds. It can have significant benefits, both in cash and by reducing the stress on the income provider. By following the steps below and using a cash flow spreadsheet you should be able to create a useful cash flow report.

Check the report against actual transactions each month to ensure the data is current and accurate.

> *A cash flow is not a precise document, and it doesn't matter if it changes, provided you learn and improve as you go along.*

Creating a Cash Flow report:
1. Determine how much money you have now.
2. Enter monthly income actually received (this may not be the same amount as the budget income).
3. Enter expenses in the month they are actually paid (this may not be equal the month budget, but it should equal the total budget amount).
4. Calculate monthly net cash flow (total income less total expenses for the month).
5. Calculate the month's closing cash position (opening cash less monthly net cash flow). Transfer this amount to the next month's opening cash position.
6. Review the cash flow position for future months.

If the cash flow statement shows a negative closing amount, you will need to find money in order to pay all your expenses. Perhaps it is possible to move a bill to another month (insurance).

You can start a cash flow from a budget—or you may use the cash flow to create a budget.

Chapter 17

Cash Flow Example:

Using the figures from the budget section, below is the summary of how they appear in the cash flow.

Account	Budget	January	February	March	April
Opening Cash		$275	$1,126	$1,559	$2,686
Income					
Wages	$56,238	$4,326	$4,326	$5,407	$4,326
Interest	$102	0	0	$51	0
Total Income	$56,340	$4,326	$4,326	$5,457	$4,326
Expense					
Bank fees	$78	$6	$6	$6	$6
Electricity	$1,672	0	$418	0	0
Food	$11,000	$1,000	$1,000	$1,250	$1,000
Insurance	$375	0	0	0	$375
Medical	$500	0	0	0	0
Car costs	$4,920	$340	$340	$425	$340
Rent	$21,840	$1,680	$1,680	$2,100	$1,680
Sundry	$5,200	$400	$400	$500	$400
Telephone	$599	$49	$49	$49	$49
Total Expense	$46,184	$3,475	$3,893	$4,330	$3,850
Cash		$851	$433	$1,127	$476
Surplus	$10,156				
End Cash		$1,126	$1,559	$2,686	$3,162

Cash flow

I have made the following assumptions:

Wages is currently $1,050 plus a rise of 3% = $1,081 per week. In January, February, and April there are 4 weeks and there are 5 weeks in March.

Interest is received twice a year; I have put half the budget amount in March.

Bank fees were easy at $6 each month.

Electricity is only quarterly. I have divided the annual amount by 4 and entered one quarter in February, which is when the next bill is due.

Food is by the week and works the same as wages.

Insurance is due in April; the full amount is included in that month.

There are no ***medical*** bills at the moment; the cash flow shows nil.

Motor Vehicles include fuel; service is not due in this period.

Rent and ***Sundry*** is per week and apportioned like wages.

Telephone is per month.

The *cash movement* for the month is the total income less the total expenses.

The *closing cash balance* is the opening balance plus the cash movement. The closing cash balance for January becomes the opening cash balance for February and so on. As the cash movement each month is positive, the closing cash balance is increasing. This does not always occur; it may go up and down during the year.

Chapter 17

Functions of a Cash Flow Report

If we see when the cash is coming into the bank and when it is going out of the bank we are able to make decisions about what to do with the balance.

At the end of April there should be over $3,000 in the bank account; perhaps it is time to think about moving some of these funds to a term deposit to earn better interest.

Perhaps it is time to repay a loan or even to buy something for the house. As you expand this cash flow to include the full year, you will know when you have money and when you will need to subsidise the cash flow.

If there is a cash flow deficit (*negative amount*) during the year, it is time to consider how to will fund it—perhaps with a loan or from savings. Being aware of when the money will run out gives you time to plan, obtain funds at the best price and time, and

be in control of your money.

Chapter 18

Tax

How the Government Earns Money

Governments need money to operate services around the country:

- Health
- Education
- Welfare
- Military
- Infrastructure

Taxation is the most common method the government uses to produce money to pay for these services. Taxes vary from country to country and state to state. They are applied to many different transactions and people.

The Australian personal income taxation system is based on self-assessment. You are responsible for working out how much income you earn and what deductions you can claim. The information provided by people to the tax office is initially accepted as true and accurate. The Australian Taxation Office (ATO) may, at a later date, ask to see written evidence to substantiate this information; accurate records should be kept for up to 5 years from the end of the tax year. Asset and loan entries need to be kept for 5 years from the final transaction. For example 5 years after a car is sold—not from when it was purchased. If you are unable to provide these records, your returns may be adjusted and charges and interest may be applied—even though the tax return had been originally accepted.

In Australia, the tax year runs from 1 July to 30 June. Tax is calculated on an annual basis, and tables showing the amount of tax to be deducted from each pay are produced by using the following calculations.

> Weekly tax = annual tax / 52
> Fortnightly tax = annual tax / 26
> Monthly tax = annual tax / 12

Tax is payable on your *taxable income,* which is the total or gross amount you receive from earnings *(including all deductions from your pay)* less allowable deductions and rebates. Tax is calculated by using a scale. The tax scales are reviewed during the preparation of the national budget; any changes to the tax scales come into place on 1 July each year.

Taxable Income = Gross Income minus Allowable Deductions minus Rebates.

Tax payable = Taxable Income x Tax rate.

Tax adjustment = the difference between what is calculated on an annual basis and the tax you have paid during the year.

Tax paid can be in the form of deductions from your pay or regular payments directly to the ATO.

Taxable Income

Taxable income includes most types of money you receive less allowable deductions and rebates as described by the tax office. A full list of income can be found on the ATO website. This includes wages paid by an employer, subcontractor payments, interest received on your bank account, government payments, and investment income.

Tax Deductions

You can claim a tax deduction if you spend money that is directly related to earning your income. You cannot claim normal private expenses. You are required by the tax department to keep evidence of these expenses (usually a tax invoice) and prove how it is needed by you to earn your income. You cannot claim a deduction for an expense you have not paid. It must be related to earning your income. Common deductions are:

- ✓ Work-related car and travel expenses. This does not include normal travel to and from work, but it does include trips performed for work-related activities while you are at work.
- ✓ Work-related clothing, uniforms, and dry-cleaning or laundry expenses to maintain special clothing.

> *If you are required to wear safety boots for your job, you can claim the cost of the boots as a tax deduction. However, if you are a professional and like to wear a suit to work, this cost will most likely be denied as "not being required to earn your income" because you can perform you job and earn income equally well in your normal clothes.*

- ✓ Gifts or donations to ATO-approved organizations (see the ATO website for approved organizations).
- ✓ Education expenses—if they are connected to your current employment. If they are for a new career, they may not be claimed as a tax deduction until you actually earn an income in that career.

> *If you are studying to become an engineer, but you currently work at a Pizza parlour, you cannot claim the course costs as a deduction.*

- ✓ Cost of managing your affairs—tax agent or accounting costs.

Allowable deductions do not include the full value of assets, unless they are under the threshold set down by the ATO. More commonly, assets should be depreciated over their useful life. Depreciation means claiming a portion of the cost of the asset in each year that it is in use. For more details visit the ATO website or ask your accountant.

Chapter 18

Helen's Tips:
- ✓ Know the rules.
- ✓ Keep in your comfort zone.
- ✓ Do not make claims you cannot support.
- ✓ Keep records.

Tax Payable

For full-time, part-time and casual employees, tax is deducted from your pay and forwarded to the tax office by the employer. These payments are called pay-as-you-go (PAYG) withholdings.

If you do not receive a regular salary or wage you may be making direct contributions to the ATO. These may be included in your Business Activity Statement (BAS) and are called pay-as-you-go (PAYG) instalments.

Sometimes in your life you may have the opportunity to vary the amount of tax you pay. More information can be found in chapter 25.

Annual Tax Return and Tax Adjustment

At the end of the financial year (30 June), taxpayers are asked to complete a tax return to show the total income earned and total tax already paid for the year. There is often an adjustment required, which can be money refunded or required to be paid to the tax office. Refunds are paid directly to your bank account. If there is an amount to be paid, this will be included in the assessment notice, and you will be given a short time to pay the funds to the tax office. If you have difficulty paying the tax, you should contact the ATO as soon as possible to discuss repayment options. The tax office can be flexible; however, there is provision in the tax act for the ATO to charge fines and interest for late payments or non-payment.

Helen's Tip:

Understand your tax position. Be prepared for the assessment amount. Don't ignore payment advices from the tax office.

Tips for a Better Tax Return

- ✓ Always lodge on time—organize yourself and your paperwork in line with the tax year—*in Australia July 1 to June 30*. Individual tax returns are due by 31 October each year; however, some people are allowed extensions by lodging their tax return with an accountant.
- ✓ Keep all documents and records—(receipts and tax invoices). Note all payments without receipts (donations). List your transactions to make it easier to complete the tax return.

Your memory is not good enough!

- ✓ Read about deductions available in the tax information guide each year to understand the types of deductions you can claim. These can change from year to year.
- ✓ Include all income. Do not leave yourself open for audit or assessment; the tax office does a lot of data matching—(bank interest, government grants etc.).

- ✓ Split income if you are able—between partners, siblings, or children to produce a lower taxable income and pay less tax.
- ✓ Check calculations for tax payments on the website and ensure you include the Medicare levy. Prepare for the resulting payment or refund amount.
- ✓ Do it yourself or with a friend or partner. By understanding the tax system, you will be able to take advantage of all tax rules.
- ✓ Lodge on line. This is faster since it doesn't need to be entered by an ATO staff member. You will also receive any refunds quicker.

PAYG and Tax Tables

Pay as you go (PAYG) withholding tax is deducted from your pay by the employer and paid to the ATO. This means part of your pay is actually going straight to the government before you see it.

The Australian tax system is based on a tax scale; the more money you earn, the higher tax rate you will pay. Currently in Australia there is a tax free threshold ($18,200) which means that every individual can earn up to this amount and not pay any tax. After this amount, tax is applied to every dollar of taxable income. There are 5 thresholds in the full tax tables, and it is worth knowing the ones that are close to your income.

Tax

For the year 1 July 2012 to 30 June 2013 the individual tax rates are:

$0 - $18,200	Nil
$18,201 - $37,000	19 cents for each $1 over $18,200
$37,001 - $80,000	$3,572 plus 32.5 cents for each $1 over $37,000
$80,00 - $180,000	$17,547 plus 37 cents for each $1 over $80,000
$180,000 and over	$54,547 plus 45 cents for each $1 over $180,000

These rates do not include the Medicare levy as it is not added to all individuals' tax rates.

For future rates go to the ATO website and find Individual Income Tax Rates.

Every income earner should know 2 things about their tax rates:

1. What is your marginal tax rate?
2. At what income level will the marginal rate change?

Your marginal tax rate is the amount of tax applied to your last dollar earned. This is different from the amount of tax applied to your first dollar earned, which is nil, because of the tax-free threshold.

Chapter 18

Tax calculation Example

If you are employed on a regular basis and earn $40,000 per year, you fall into the tax rate of $37,001 - $80,000. Your marginal tax rate is 32.5 cents per dollar; it is the rate that is applied to every *extra* dollar you earn. The rate will change when your taxable income goes over $80,000 to 37 cents per dollar.

Tax is calculated as follows:	
0 - $18,200	Nil
$18,201 - $37,000 x 19 cents =	$3,572
$37,001 - $40,000 x 32.5 cents =	$975
Total tax payable for the year =	**$4,547**

The average amount of tax you have paid is calculated by dividing the total tax by your total earnings. For example, $40,000 / $4,547 = 11 cents per dollar.

If you earn $41,000 per year, your tax is calculated as follows:

$0 - $18,200	Nil
$18,201 - $37,000 x 19 cents =	$3,572
$37,000 - $40,000 x 32.5 cents =	$975
$40,000 - $41,000 x 32.5 cents =	$325
Total tax payable for the year =	**$4,872**

Now the average tax is 12 cents per dollar earned.
Average tax will change as your taxable income changes.

The tax scales are designed to ensure lower-paid workers pay lower taxes and higher-paid earners pay more taxes. The extra amount you earned ($1,000) is taxed at the marginal rate of 32.5 cents = $325. And your full-year tax has gone up to $4,872.

Helen's Tip:

Know what your marginal rate is and when it changes.

Different Types of Tax

Income Tax

The amount of tax individuals pay is based on the income he or she earns.

Company Tax

Companies pay tax on every dollar of profit they make. This is different from individual income tax. It is a flat rate and applies from the first dollar of profit and to all profit dollars. The current company tax rate is 30 cents per dollar.

Medicare Levy

The Medicare levy and Medicare levy surcharge are amounts added to an individual's taxes. The levy is specifically collected to fund medical and hospital care. Currently the Medicare levy is 1.5%. This changes the above tax thresholds for the year 1 July 2012 to 30 June 2013 to:

$0 - $18,200	Nil
$18,201 - $37,000	20.5 cents
$37,001 - $80,000	34 cents
$80,001 - $180,000	38.5 cents
$180,000 and over	46.5 cents

The Medicare levy surcharge is applied to income earners above a threshold who don't have private hospital coverage. The surcharge is currently an additional 1%.

Capital Gains Tax

Capital Gains Taxes started 21 September 1985 and are applicable when an asset is purchased and sold for a profit after this date. The capital gains are calculated by taking the selling price less the purchase price and any costs and improvements. If you own the asset for more than 12 months there is a discount of 50% of the capital gains. For assets purchased between 21 September 1985 and 20 September 1999, the indexation or discount method can be used.

Goods and Services Tax

Goods and Services Tax (GST) is a broad-based tax. It was implemented in Australia in 2000. It is called a broad-based tax because it is levied on most goods and services. In order to avoid a double or accumulating tax from applying, the government refunds the GST paid by companies on goods and services needed to operate their companies. This means only the end user pays the tax on the final value of the item. In Australia, the GST must be included in the advertised sales price to simplify buying for the consumer. For every sale, 1/11 of the value is remitted to the tax office by the company selling the goods or services. Many countries have a similar tax system but it is known by different names:

UK	VAT—value added tax
European Union	VAT—value added tax
Japan	Consumption tax
New Zealand	GST—Goods and Services Tax

The current rate of GST in Australia is 10%.

Land Tax

Land Tax is calculated on the value of all land, other than your residential home, as assessed by the local government. It varies state to state. It is like council rates; an annual notice will be sent out that shows the total amount payable. It can then be paid in one payment or in quarterly instalments.

Stamp Duties

Stamp duties or taxes are applied by the state governments on certain documents and transactions. Duties are paid to lodge these documents. For instance, when you transfer a motor vehicle or a house from one person to another, a document describing the transfer needs to be lodged with the state government. They will keep a record of the name of the legal owner. Duty is paid for every document and can range from a fixed amount to a percentage of the value. Since this is a state tax, check the individual state websites for rates.

Chapter 18

Fringe Benefits Tax

The Fringe Benefits Tax was first introduced in Australia in 1986. It is a tax payable by the employer on the value of the fringe benefit the employee receives. Instead of paying the employee cash and applying tax, superannuation etc., the employer provides a benefit.

Annual tax returns are prepared by each company April 1 to March 31. First, a dollar value is placed on the benefit and then the tax rate is applied, which increases its value—this is called the "grossed-up value" of the benefit. The "grossed-up value" of the benefit is shown on the annual payment summaries provided to the employee at the end of the financial year.

Note: the fringe benefit reporting year and annual payment summary reporting year do not match. Fringe benefits paid during the year April 1 to 31 March, are included with annual payment summary for the year 1 July to 30 June.

Wine Equalization Tax

This is a tax placed on wine only. It is added to the cost of wine and the manufacturer submits the total to the tax office. Before the GST was bought in, wine had a large sales tax applied. Without the wine equalization tax, the cost of wine would have been reduced significantly. This was thought unfavourable by the government; therefore, when the broad-based GST was bought into Australia and sales was tax removed, the wine equalization tax was introduced. The tax is shown on the Business Activity Statement and paid to the tax office at the same time as GST payments, so more people are aware of it than with the previous sales tax system. Wine Equalisation Tax only affects a small number of companies.

Luxury Car Tax

As with the wine equalization tax, the luxury car tax was bought into Australia in 2000 with the GST. It is a tax on vehicles priced over the threshold, which is subject to change. Luxury car tax is primarily applied and collected by the original seller of a new car. Like the wine equalization tax, the luxury car tax is remitted to the tax office with the GST and thus is more widely known.

Payroll Tax

Payroll tax is a state tax that is only paid by companies whose annual payroll amount exceeds the state threshold. It is paid on top of company tax and PAYG tax. The rate of tax changes from state to state and can change from year to year. Consult the website for each state's tax rates.

Tax Evasion

Why do people evade taxes? To save the individual money.

Why should people not evade taxes?—To save the country and your fellow workers.

> If everyone evaded taxes there would be no money to run the country.

By avoiding taxes the burden to run the country is carried by those who do not avoid taxes.

Tax avoidance is against the law and carries heavy fine and penalties.

Chapter 19

Review

Take a Look at Previous Money Decisions

Once upon a time, children grew up on milo and homemade chocolate chip cookies and went to school until year 10 or 12. They then went to work or university. They got married in their 20's and went to the bank for a 20-25 year loan to buy a house. They had 2.5 children (*I never really understood how to have .5 of a child!*) and lived happily ever after.

Money wise this story works well as these people reached their mid-40's, paid off their home loans and owned their own houses. They could then accumulate money to travel or bought a few luxuries before saving for retirement. The government pension was able to fund your retirement; as your children became parents, you became grandparents and lived a long, successful life.

What changed?

> ➢ Children drink coke—not milo—and eat take out foods instead of cookies. Both cost more!

Review

- People don't get married in their 20's and often do not wait until they are married to buy a house.
- Children are being born much later in life. The cost of raising children continues later in the parents' lives.
- The standard 25 year housing loan is quite rare; it has been replaced by much more flexible loans and redraw facilities. Loans are not being paid off before retirement age.
- We all want to travel more, buy the latest television and drive the newest cars.

Our expectations are higher.

- When we retire, the government pension will not be available to everyone—and it may not support your current lifestyle.
- There is much more competition in the marketplace, both locally and overseas.

Our world is full of options!

- What university? What course? What line of education?
- Which employers? What jobs? What locations?
- Stay single? Get married? Live together?
- Have children—or don't?
- Buy? Rent? Live at home?
- Travel? Buy possessions? Enjoy a lifestyle.

Chapter 19

Change is a fact of life—and it is occurring faster than ever before!

- Communications
- Computers
- Finance
- Education
- Medical research and advancements
- Government operations

Our rapidly changing world provides many more options. It is becoming increasingly necessary to *review* decisions you have made more often. There are better, cheaper, faster, and more efficient ways of doing just about everything now—and many of these options are available to everyday people.

What to review?

- Home loans.
- Other loans—car, furniture, or holiday loans.
- Credit cards.
- Insurance policies.
- Health coverage.
- Cars—ownership, maintenance, insurance.
- Utilities (telephone, electricity, water).

Review the above items and ensure you have:

- ✓ The Best Interest Rates.
- ✓ Flexible Terms.
- ✓ Suitable Repayment Amounts.
- ✓ Features Suitable for your Personal Situation.

Review

- ✓ Suitable limits.
- ✓ Appropriate Coverage and Inclusions.

Watch out for hidden fees or terms on payout or transfer.

When do you need to review?

Most money decisions should be reviewed annually. Loans can be longer term and therefore reviewed at the end of the loan. Very long loans (housing) should be reviewed every few years of it you other circumstances change.

Review Methods

- ➢ Ensure records are easy to find *(see Chapter 21 Filing).*
- ➢ Keep a review sheet that only requires a tick or a cross entry *(see review sheet in the back of the book).*
- ➢ Try to line up all policies to mature at the same time. Your cash flow may need you to divide the premium payments throughout the year.

> *Review health insurance, personal insurance, and superannuation in December and household insurance policies in June. Car insurance can be done in March and car registrations in September. Utilities occur monthly and can be reviewed in December or June.*

- ➢ Select a couple of competing companies to compare with your current arrangement.

> Start by asking if you still need this arrangement. If yes, then compare. If no, cancel it and save the money.

How do you choose which companies to use in a review?

Ask friends and work colleagues about the companies they use; however, be aware that advice from your family will contain similar views to your own—and you may want different opinions.

Ask people for the following advice:

> Who is your insurance with?
> Why did you choose this company?
> Would you recommend them?
> If you are comfortable with discussing money, you may also ask for the financial information on cost and benefits of the policy.

Once you find another company to compare your existing arrangements with, keep notes on why you have made your current selection. This will help with future comparisons.

Helen's Tip:

Regularly reviewing your financial contracts will make the process easier.

Start now and get ahead with financial management.

Chapter 20

Insurance

Money Saved with an Insurance Company Is Repaid to the Customer in the Case of Disaster

Consider insurance as your fall-back plan in case things go wrong. You need insurance if you could not afford to replace the item if it was taken away?

> ➢ Can you afford to buy a new home if your current home was destroyed?
> ➢ Can you afford to buy a replacement car if your current car was destroyed?
> ➢ Can you afford to pay the medical bills if you become sick?
> ➢ What happens if you are disabled or permanently unwell?

Insurance is a binding agreement between you and the insurance company that is renewed each year. This agreement remains in place while the premiums are paid. The onus is on the person taking out the insurance to ensure the premiums are fully paid—and not the insurance company.

Buying insurance

When inquiring about insurance, you will need to consider the following items:

- Value—or payout figure in the case of a claim.
- Cost—premiums can be paid annually or monthly.
- Terms—limitations on when a claim can be made or special conditions to make a claim.
- Coverage—exactly what is included and what is not included.
- Company reputation and convenience of payments, queries and claims.
- Excess—there may be an amount you have to pay before the insurance company starts to pay.

Sum Insured

The maximum an insurer will pay you, on a claim is the "sum insured" as shown on the contract. This amount has to cover everything you want replaced.

Some policies also offer inconvenience charges, such as towing a car or a paying for a place to stay. These extras can become necessary if you travel away from home a lot.

It is a juggling act between how much you want as the sum insured and how much you want to pay in the premium. Comparing quotes will help you make the best decisions for your circumstances at the time.

Paperwork

Once you have decided on the insurance policy, there will be paperwork to be completed. Ensure that all details are accurate and not misleading since this will hinder a claim. Remember to update your details if your personal circumstances change.

Payment

Insurance premiums can be paid annually on a reminder notice or by regular instalments throughout the year. If you do not pay the premium (even if you did not receive a notice to pay) you may not be covered. An insurance schedule will help remind you when premiums are due.

Monthly payments often suit the cash flow; however, this can cost more and increase the overall annual amount.

Some insurance premiums are tax deductable if they are considered necessary to earn your income. Life insurance attached to a superannuation fund is tax effective.

Making a Claim

Step 1: Contact the Insurance Company.

When you want to make a claim—or even if you think you want to make a claim—on an insurance policy, it is very important to contact the insurance company *as soon as possible*. This cannot be emphasized strongly enough.

Many people forget to inform insurance companies, file a claim too late, or forget all the facts. As soon as possible after the event, contact the insurance company and let them know something has happened—and you are or may be making a claim. The insurance company will keep track of your claim, and the process will be easier and quicker than if you delay first contact.

Step 2: Allow time for your claim to be processed.

It is also important to discuss the claims process with the insurance company. Do there need to be any inspections? By whom? When? This should be done before you start organizing clean-ups, towing, repairs, or assistance. Do not assume all insurance companies are the same.

> *Just because your friend's insurance company paid for the carpets to be replaced does not mean the same will be true for you.*

Keep in contact with your insurance company during the process and until fully complete.

Types of Insurance

- Home or building—*protects a building and things attached to the building.*
- Contents—*protects things inside the building that are not attached to the building.*
- Personal Property—*coverage for personal belongings while they are outside of the house (camera equipment and jewellery).*
- Motor Vehicle—*protects a car, bike, truck or piece of equipment.*
- Boat—*protects a boat, attachments and contents.*

- Trailer—*protects a trailer.*
- Life—*protects the life of a person.* The benefit is received by another person (the beneficiary) on death.
- Disability—*protects against various types of accidents and diseases.*
- Income protection—*pays money regularly if you are unable to work.*
- Public liability—*insures claims by a member of the public for injury incurred on your property or place of business.*
- Workers compensation—*taken out by businesses, it protects workers against injury while they are at work, or travelling to or from work.*
- Health—*provides financial assistance for medical costs.*
- Business—*protects the business from different types of disasters.*
- Travel—*insures people while travelling against medical problems, loss of belongings and unforeseeable changes to travelling arrangements.*
- Landlord—*protects home owners from tenant damage or loss of income.* This separate policy is designed for investors since many standard house and contents policies do not cover the landlord's risks.
- Mortgage—*protects the lender against non-payment of a loan.* This insurance is often needed when the mortgage is a high percentage of the value of the house.

Helen's Tip:

Keep track of your insurance policies to keep covered for life.

Insurance

To Reduce Insurance Premiums

- Adequately maintain houses and cars.
- Install smoke detectors.
- Ensure good electrical wiring.
- Install window and door locks.
- Consider burglar alarms and security devices.
- An accident-free driving record.
- Linking policies—superannuation funds with life, disability, and sickness insurance.
- Reducing the value from purchase price to market value.
- Covering only specific destinations.
- Annual travel insurance if you travel more than 3 times per year.
- Keeping all family members on one policy.
- Reducing policy members as the children reach maturity age.
- Only insure employees, and request subcontractors have their own insurance.

Chapter 21

Filing

Sorting the Shoebox

Helen's Tip:

I hate filing, but I hate not being able to find something more!

Filing tips

- Deal with every piece of paper as soon as you get it.
- Recycle unnecessary mail and paper as soon as possible.
- Have an in tray and a bills tray to sort paperwork as soon as it is received.
- Put everything in a filing tray when you have finished working on it.
- Set a certain time in your week or month to empty the filing tray.
- Never let the filing tray overflow. Not only is this a large amount of filing to do, but papers can fall out.
- Establish a working filing system for regular bills, invoices, etc. and a long-term filing system for loan or rental agreements, insurances, taxes etc.
- Every year, remove all the paper work that relates to the tax year from the working files and store it for a minimum of 5 years.
- File in the same order—whether that is alphabetical or numerical, monthly or yearly.
- Empty tissue boxes work well for receipts in cars and trucks. Put all papers in the box so they won't fly away. Transfer receipts to the working file regularly.
- Label all files to prevent misuse—a bill to be paid should never be placed in the filing tray!

Filing Methods

Your filing system will depend on the quantity of paper and the ease you need to get to it. If you need the information all the time, it needs to be in good order. The following are some options for filing:

✓ A-Z expanding folder. This is good for bills and invoices, but only if you can get a full year in one file. Each year, you need to buy new file and start again. Alphabetical works well if there are only one or two people using the filing system. It does not work as well if there are many users because each user can file under a different name, making finding the paperwork difficult.

> *For example, The Weekly Paper bill can be filed under $\underline{T}$ for The or $\underline{W}$ for Weekly or $\underline{P}$ for Paper bill?*

✓ A filing cabinet or an archive box with loose leaf manila folders is good for long-term filing (insurance, cars, loans, medical, wills). Use separate folders for each item and then store them in alphabetical order.

✓ An A4 book or folder with see-through plastic sleeves is great for reference information that you need to access all the time (loan schedules, insurance summaries, budgets).

✓ Ring folders with dividers keep papers from falling out and work well if you have a lot of papers (bank statements, or invoices). It is common to need the most recent statements first; filing them on top, rather than underneath, ensures easy access.

✓ Chits or small pieces of paper (credit card receipts)can most easily be filed in envelopes, labelled for each week or month they relate to.

✓ Dockets printed on thermal paper will fade. If the information is important or needs to be kept, photocopying them will ensure the details are preserved.

Filing

Keeping Records

People keep records for following reasons;

- Personal information
- Tax support documentation
- Legal necessity
- Business records

Personal Information

People choose to keep documents for reference, information, or sentimental reasons. In order to be useful, they need to be readily available and easy to find; however, what you keep is a personal decision. Don't decide to keep every piece of paper you own; some papers should be thrown away. Keeping unnecessary paperwork will only clutter your filing system. Always keep personal paper-work separate from tax and legal documents to ensure they are not discarded by mistake.

Tax Documentation

If your tax return is selected for review, you will have to provide receipts or extra information to support your claims. All documents must be in writing (not on a computer) and in English (unless the expense was incurred outside Australia). All records need to be kept for 5 years from the date of tax lodgement.

Separate each financial year. At the end of June, clean out all last year's records and put them in a box that is clearly labelled with the corresponding dates (2012-2013 tax year). Most importantly, keep a copy of your tax return, the assessment notice, and any communication with the tax office—together and in date order.

You need to keep certain documents for tax purposes.

Income:

- Payment summaries (also called group certificates) and payslips.
- Rental summaries covering any rental income received.
- Bank statements showing interest received—most banks now summarise the total received for the year under the 30 June transactions.
- Government allowances, grants, or pension amounts. You will receive a statement from the Government detailing these amounts.
- Superannuation—your superannuation fund should send a statement annually.
- Support for any other type of income that has been shown on the tax return.

Allowances and Deductions:

- Written evidence of travel expenses (invoices and receipts).
- Rental expenses for investment properties (rates notices, repair bills, and maintenance invoices).
- If you claim an expense against an allowance you have received (travel, uniform, or tools), there is no need to keep written evidence—provided it is for the same amount of the allowance. If you wish to claim a higher deduction amount than you received as an allowance, you will need written evidence. To be on the safe side, keep all documents recording the expense and discuss this with your tax advisor.
- Many people forget the small amounts they pay during the working year (bus fares, train or tram tickets, bridge or road tolls, and parking fees). If you have the receipt, it will remind you of the expense. You can discuss whether

it is an allowable deduction with your accountant. If you do not get a receipt, keep a diary record at the time of the event rather than trying to remember later. Record dates, places, times, duration of activities, and amounts paid.

Legal Documents

In legal disputes, written evidence may be needed as proof of action. Computers, although very useful, do not take the place of a hard copy because computer programs, users, passwords, and logins can change, and access to the original information may no longer be available.

Types of documents kept for legal purposes:

- Proof of asset purchase and sale.
- Loans and lease agreements (and any other documents you have signed).

Business Documents

Certain business documents need to be kept:

- Documents for tax preparation. *See above.*
- Documents specific to the business and its operations (manuals, customer and supplier details).
- Financial reports, including Profit and Loss Statements and Balance Sheets that show the business operations.
- Asset and equipment records.
- Stock records.
- Advertising and marketing materials.

When a business is to be sold, the accuracy of business records will assist a profitable sale.

Chapter 22

Business

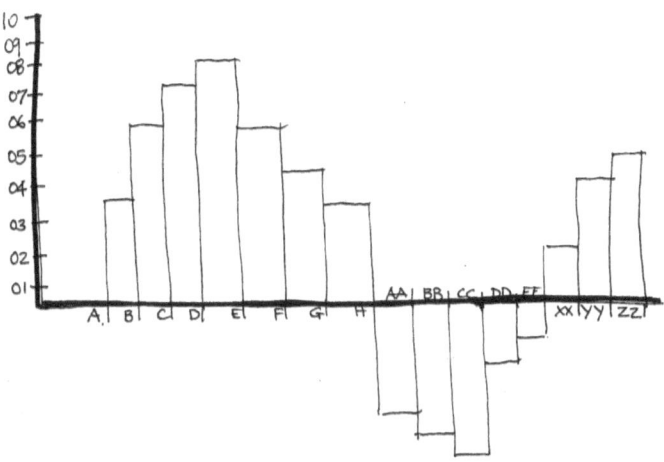

If you are running a business, there are a number of extra money matters to consider and manage. Unfortunately, many people become business owners because they are good at their profession; however, this does not mean they are good at managing money in a business.

I have briefly listed the main areas to consider when going into business; however, the assistance of a business advisor should also be sought.

Time

Most first-time small business owners are shocked at the time involved to complete business paperwork and compliance items. Time spent in the early days researching what is needed to run a small business—both in start-up systems and ongoing compliance—is time saved at the end of the first reporting period. Shoe box accounting is a thing of the past since the GST and introduction of regular reporting in 2000. Know what you are getting yourself into, ask for help, and do it right at the beginning to save time and heartache later on.

Taxes

Most businesses now pay tax quarterly with a Business Activity Statement (BAS), although some small businesses are able to pay taxes annually. In order to produce the BAS statements, your record keeping must be up to date and in a format for extracting the necessary information. It also means understanding a lot more about the tax system, including GST, PAYG withholding, PAYG instalments, and other industry-specific taxes.

Although it is possible to hand this area of your business over to an accountant, operating any business without a sound understanding on how taxation works is not wise.

Taxes are a cost and need to be budgeted for by every business owner.

Chapter 22

Receiving Funds

When you go into business for yourself, you will need to provide documentation to your customers in order to get paid. Consider who will prepare, add up, calculate the taxes, and issue invoices. Decide who will track the payments and who will chase people who owe you money. Many business owners start off with hand written books that can be purchased from the local newsagency. However, this is time consuming and less professional than computer-generated invoices. Manual systems do not leave room for expansion and are subject to human error. It is easier and cleaner to set it up a computerised accounting system from the beginning.

Tax Invoices

The most common document used in business today is the tax invoice. This document is used to pay a supplier. You create a tax invoice for your customers to pay you. There are certain requirements for a tax invoice to be valid, including name, address, Australian Business Number (ABN), date, details of the charges, and whether or not GST is included. Tax invoices can then be customised to suit the business needs.

> *Many businesses now include bank details to enable direct debit of payments.*

Paying People

Your reputation is often created by the manner in which you pay your accounts. Do you pay them regularly or only when chased? Credit checks are still performed by many companies; without a good credit reference, you will find it difficult to obtain further credit.

The rules for business finance are the same as personal finance.

Do not spend what you do not have.

It is efficient to pay all bills on one day rather than every day of the month. A 30 day account system is common, although some companies are trying to break this practice and ask for payment in 7 or 14 days or on delivery.

Many businesses have implemented a discount system if the invoices are paid by a certain date; taking advantage of this system can save a company a lot of money. Investigate and use wherever practical.

Insurance

When you operate a small business, you will need more types of insurance. Public liability, worker's compensation, loss of trading, and building and equipment insurances should be investigated. Many insurance companies are able to bundle policies into one general business policy.

Advertising and Marketing

Without advertising, it will be difficult to grow your business. There are many advertising and marketing ideas available; consider where your business is going to come from, now and in the future, and direct your advertising at these markets. Seek expert advice and ask lots of questions.

Chapter 22

Staying Current

We live in an ever-changing world—and change is occurring faster than ever before. Business owners need to keep up to date with changes in your industry, business in general, government compliance, and taxation changes. Subscriptions to magazines, seminars, conferences, online research sessions and user groups are all useful ways to stay informed.

Employees

Employees can make or break any business. They should be thought of as a valuable asset to be nurtured and looked after. Employees require training and support throughout their employment. This costs money; invest wisely and try to reduce staff turnover.

<u>Helen's Tip:</u>
What goes around comes around.

Employees can be the bane of a business, causing headaches and heartaches. There are a lot of legal and taxation compliance issues around employing people; the rules are continually changing as governments, unions, and standards change. It is often difficult to try to manage employees by yourself; you may need to employ a team or a Human Resources department to manage and be responsible for all

employee issues. It is wise for business owners and managers to know their employees and understand their personal situations. Be there and be aware—but keep your distance and leave compliance to the experts.

Business versus Personal

Business and personal transactions can become entwined. The following steps are advised for those who operate their own business:

- Open a bank account in the name of the business—separate from your personal bank account.
- Ensure all business expenses are paid by the business account.
- Make sure your staff understands how your business and personal systems work and how they are separated.
- Keep all documents in an organised filing system. Business documents stay separate from personal documents.
- Get into the habit of keeping your records up to date, preferably daily (business) or weekly (personal).
- Back up business data on a regular basis.
- Talk to an accountant before the start of trading to ensure systems meet their needs and costs can be kept to a minimum.
- Keep a diary.

Chapter 23

Fringe Benefits

Something Besides Money You Are Able To Use

A fringe benefit is anything—except money—that an employee receives from an employer.

Every job has fringe benefits of some kind. Employees and employers need to recognize them and determine how much they are worth to them in time, money, or flexibility.

Fringe benefits mean different things to different people.

Helen's Tip:

Never underestimate the true value of a fringe benefit.

Fringe Benefits

> *Some examples are:*
>
> - *Use of a car for personal trips, parking.*
> - *Business Travel—this can be an advantage or a disadvantage if it takes you away from your family.*
> - *Entertainment—dinners, lunches, morning teas, drinks, or recreation (playing golf). If the employee is attending a conference, training, business trip or activity, it is not considered a fringe benefit.*
> - *Meals—provided by employer.*
> - *Uniforms.*
> - *Use of a house or accommodation owned by the employer.*
> - *Allowances above the reasonable amounts set down by the Australian Taxation Office (see ATO website for the reasonable amounts as they change regularly).*
> - *Flexible hours.*
> - *Debts waived or not required to be paid in full.*

The benefits can be apportioned between a personal benefits and a work related expense.

> *If 50% of the use of the company car is for business and 50% is for personal use, then only the personal usage percentage is classified as fringe benefits; the rest is a business expense.*

The way expenses are proportioned can depend on the time spent carrying out business to personal work, usage, mileage and who is involved, for instance, if a partner or family is on the trip.

> Many jobs offer a range of fringe benefits that employees do not recognise: tea, coffee, biscuits, stationery products, discounts, vouchers to use in the business, or a Christmas gift.

Fringe Benefits tax returns are completed by the company and are reported on the individual employee's payment summary each year. Gifts of less than $100 are exempt from fringe benefits tax—as are electronic diaries, personal organizers, briefcases, tools and tool boxes used in the business, laptop computers, and business or trade magazine subscriptions.

Employees who receive a payment summary with a fringe benefit amount shown should ask their employer to supply the calculations for this amount and keep it with their tax records.

Fringe benefits are not taxable for the individual; however, they may adjust some government benefits or be used to assess loan and financial status.

Certain religious and community businesses are able to pay employees an equivalent higher package using fringe benefits.

Chapter 24

Holidays

Time Away From Work

We all need regular holidays to rest and rejuvenate. Holidays offer a reward for working hard and a break from day-to-day living.

Some people have adventure holidays, and some choose to relax! Whatever type of holiday you like, take at least one holiday every year. Your work, family, and friends will love to hear about your trip—and you will settle and work better after a break. This is why annual leave is part of standard employment conditions.

Holidays can also show you different communities and cultures. Seeing how others live, work, and play gives you a different perspective on life.

Holidays

When and where is your next holiday?
And the one after that?
And the dream one you have been planning forever?

Helen's Tip:

If you don't plan it—it will never happen—start planning your next holiday today!

Guidelines to planning a holiday.

- It takes *time to arrange* a big holiday. Give yourself enough time to get all the details just right.
- Plan *different types* of holidays—weekends away, camping, 5-star holidays, beaches, boating, shopping, relaxing, family, touring, getaways and overseas.
- *Pay for the holiday in advance.* Do not borrow to book a holiday. Repaying the holiday costs—as well as the spending money—can be a lot once you return from the trip. The memory often fades quicker than the bills do!
- There are 3 *big cost* holiday items: travel, accommodations, and meals. Look at these items first, particularly if you are on a budget. Review and cost each item and spend your money where *you* want to. We don't all holiday in the same fashion.

Do you prefer to save money by preparing your own meals and having a hotel to stay in—or would you prefer to eat out each night but sleep in a tent!

Chapter 24

- Have a budget for *spending money* and stick to it.
- Once on holiday, you often do not return to buy that special token—so buy it now. The cost to come back is enormous.
- Carefully consider the *length* of the holiday—especially overseas holidays. Being on holidays is great, but how long do you want to be away from the comforts of home? Sometimes you can see too many churches or flower shows! Would it be better to split one holiday into different trips?
- The more you *plan*, the more you enjoy. Sometimes it is great to just go where the wind takes you. There will always be more adventure and unknown elements in a holiday than you can imagine. Therefore, plan and research the items important to *you*.

> *If sleeping in a good bed every night is important, research all the stops along the way to ensure you have a good bed. One bad night will ruin the trip for you and probably your companions.*

> *If you are picky about food, be prepared. Take supplies—just in case. If you enjoy trying different foods, extra supplies are not needed. It all depends on what you don't want to compromise on and what you are happy to go with the flow on.*

- *Holiday companions.* Being away from home and having to make decisions about unusual events, food, and accommodations can be trying on most relationships.

Tour groups often take away these problems, but they can put you with people you don't like. Small groups of friends can be good until you disagree; this can affect the whole trip. Partners often argue more when they spend all day, every day with each other.

Overseas Travel

It is now possible to travel to just about any location and do just about anything you can imagine. However, just because it is easy to get on a plane and go, take the following precautions:

- Insurance coverage for health, travel plan changes, loss of baggage, and money—is essential.
- Other countries do not have the standard of health care and may not offer it as freely as it is available in Australia. Some countries require immunisations; give yourself enough time to finish the course of medication before you go.
- Consider your medication requirements—and only take what is necessary. Understand that some countries do not allow all medications to be brought into the country. Sometimes a doctor's certificate may need to be provided.
- Water—be very careful what you drink as standards vary between countries.
- A wonderful arrangement of food will be offered to you in many different countries. You will love some and you won't love others. Be kind to your body; don't experience too much in one day.
- Cultural—from tipping to the standard of dress, ensure you know what is expected in each country you visit.

- Laws—every country makes their own laws and punishments—do not assume they are in any way the same as in Australia. They are not. Know the rules of all the countries you visit. If you break them, be prepared to suffer the consequences.
- When you travel, you are an ambassador for your home country. Behave with respect to your own country and also with respect to the countries you visit. Some things are different, but this does not make them right or wrong. Be careful who and what you criticize.
- Travel—can be long, tiring, and boring. Be prepared for the total traveling hours, not just the flying hours. You will need adequate food, water, entertainment, medical supplies and money.
- Communication is different around the world. Be prepared. Do not assume you will have the same telephone and Internet communication—at the same price—as at home.
- Customs and Immigration border control requirements are different between countries. Know what you are permitted to take into and out of each country before you visit.
- Visas—always check what legal papers you need to travel to your holiday destination. Some countries will require a valid passport (usually with 6 months remaining on it). Some will require a visa, which can take time to obtain before you go or cost local money when you arrive.

Overseas is out of this world!

Money on Holidays

Holidays can be a big cost item—or you can holiday for next to nothing. However, you often need more money on holidays than you expect for souvenirs, side trips, emergency purchases, and extras.

Money is not as readily available in every country and should not be taken for granted. Credit cards or traveller's cheques are commonly used, but do not assume they will be accepted everywhere. Always research the systems of the country you are travelling to. Take more than enough—and have a backup plan.

Automatic teller machines (ATM) are convenient, but do not rely on one card. Cash advances and foreign currency conversion fees apply *each* time you withdraw. The exchange rate will be the one the bank chooses on the day. One of the most popular products is the prepaid currency card. You can buy the card and deposit funds, which you can withdraw from ATMs. It is convenient, secure, and replaceable, but there is a fee for every transaction. You will need to know the numbers to enter because ATM keypads do not show letters.

Once you have everything arranged, booked, and packed you are ready to go. Remember to travel safely. Be careful with your belongings, money, what you eat and drink, who you talk to, and what you say.

Chapter 24

Helen's Story

My Grandmother used to send me a 5 or 10 pound notes for my birthday each year. I saved it up until I visited England many years later. Sitting at my aunt's home, she asked if we had any local currency or if we needed to go to the bank.

I proudly produced my notes and was completely floored when she said, "What is that?" It had never occurred to me that currency can change. I had old currency that was not recognized by everyday people or the shops.

It was time to find a bank! But this was easier said than done; country banks in England do not look like banks in Australia. They are often hidden in old buildings. We drove through 3 or 4 towns before realizing we would need to stop and ask for directions to a bank.

Fortunately we had time; in the end, we found a bank, exchanged the money, and withdrew more—just in case!

Chapter 25

Investing

Money spent to earn more money

"An investment in knowledge pays the best interest"
Benjamin Franklin

Knowledge is power when investing. Start gathering an understanding of what investments are—and which ones you would like to be involved in early—because becoming an expert will take time.

Investing

Investments need time to work; the sooner you start investing, the better the returns will be.

> *Destiny is not a matter of chance;*
> *it is a matter of choice.*

Investing money is a skill and many people are successful; however, equally as many are not successful and lose thousands of dollars. Money is often invested with emotion and personal consideration. However, since investments are designed to make money, money factors should be used to make decisions.

Get advice from many sources; ask professionals, friends, and business associates. Talk about what has worked, what hasn't worked, and why. Really understand the different types of investments, the risks, return, and length of the investment—or don't invest. Review every investment in full; most of all; be comfortable with where your money is going.

When you invest you will need to consider the following items, in this order:

- ✓ Capital Protection—(Risk Level)
- ✓ Term of investment
- ✓ Returns versus Growth
- ✓ Leverage
- ✓ Diversification
- ✓ Tax
- ✓ Inflation

Capital Protection

Ensuring your investment or capital is safely invested is critical to your future financial security. Investments should always be made with companies that you trust and in investment types with which you are comfortable. Chapter 1 Personality and Money, discussed risk and levels of personal comfort when dealing with money. It is critical to understand the risk related to your investment. Your comfort level should dictate which investments are best for you. Commonly, the safer your money is, the lower returns you receive. Higher returns have some level of risk.

> If it looks too good to be true it probably is too good to be true!

Terms of Investment

The length of time you want to invest is important to your investment strategy. Some investments are productive over a short period of time and some are more efficient over a longer period. How long do you want to be without this money?

Suggested investment time frames and appropriate investment choices.

How long to invest	Common Choices
6 months to 2 years	aim to earn interest with little risk e.g. term deposits
2—5 years	aim to earn mainly interest and possibly adding some growth (shares)
5 years or more	aim for capital growth as well as income (property)

Investing

The power of compounding is when you reinvest the earnings from one year to the next instead of withdrawing the earnings. Each year your principal goes up; over many years the capital amount compounds (adds) to a significant amount.

Get rich slowly!

Returns v Growth

The return on your investment is the extra income you receive from investing rather than leaving your money under the bed. Do you need a regular income from your investment? Do you have sufficient funds now but will need the regular income in the future?

Investment returns are divided into:

- ✓ Income
- ✓ Growth

Income return investments provide regular money in the form of interest, dividends, or rents. The income you receive is often called the rate of return.

Growth investments are designed to increase in value. You do not receive a regular income, but you receive a profit when the investment is sold.

Some growth investments may also provide an income, which you can balance to achieve a good overall investment.

At different times, you will require different types of investments.

Chapter 25

Leverage

Leveraging your money means using the cash you have, to borrow more money to invest. The desired outcome is that your investment is larger; hence your return or growth is larger. Of course there is a risk when you borrow any money, which must be considered when leveraging funds, because it is also possible to lose a much larger amount of money if the investment goes badly.

Diversification

Diversification means spreading your investments so you don't have all your eggs in one basket—buying investments from different investment types. The aim is to reduce the risk of losing money. If one investment produces a poor result, you still have other investments that may offset all or part of the loss.

> *This is quite common if you invest in the share market when investors can purchase shares across a range of different industries. Diversification also applies to the balance of cash, property, shares and other investments you hold.*

Tax

Whenever you earn income, it should be included in your taxable income. You will be required to pay tax at your marginal rate *(see Chapter 18 Tax)*. However the expenses you incur to earn this income are tax deductable.

Investing

Although the aim of investments is generally to produce income, there are times when the expenses are more than the income. This is called negative gearing. Income from other sources (*salary*) is reduced before calculating annual tax payable. The overall object is to reduce the taxes you pay when you are earning a high income and benefit from the investment growth later in life—when you are earning a lower income.

If you are in this situation, you can vary your regular PAYG deductions by completing the PAYG withholding variation application form available on the ATO website.

If you buy an investment, it is called an asset. When you sell this investment, there can be a profit or a loss—it is calculated as the sales price less the purchase price. If you make a profit, you will need to pay capital gains tax on any profit. There is a discount applicable if you hold the asset for more than 12 months.

Depreciation

Depreciation is a non-cash tax deduction and represents the decline in value of an asset. The ATO has published rates of depreciation; however, these can be varied depending on different types of business.

> *In some businesses, computers have a life of only 1 year. In other businesses the life may be 5 years.*

Depreciation rates are now more commonly shown as life of the assets—rather than as a percentage per year. When your investment includes assets that can be depreciated, you benefit from receiving a tax deduction as an expense, which you did not have to pay cash for.

Inflation

Inflation plays a role in choosing your investment because it changes the value of your money. The goal of investing is to increase your wealth by more than inflation. The cash you have today will drop in value over time because inflation will increase the cost of the products you can buy with the cash. Cash today will not be able to buy the same goods as in the future. Investments grow over time, trying to keep up with inflation.

> $100 today will buy you 20 cups of coffee at $5 each. If inflation is 5% per year, the cost of the coffee will go up by 5% to $5.25 in one year. At this time, you will only be able to afford 19 cups of coffee. Thus, the value of the $100 is said to have gone down.
>
> If you put the $100 in the bank and receive an interest rate of 6%, you will have $106 at the end of the year. You will be able to buy 20 cups of coffee at $5.25 each—and have $1 left over. This means your wealth has gone up (from the ability to buy 20 cups of coffee to the ability to buy 20 cups of coffee plus $1).

Doing nothing will reduce your wealth in the long term.

Investing

Types of Investment

There are many types of investments in the marketplace—below is a summary of the more common types of investments available. Some investments overlap or fall into 2 types. Exposure to risk can be reduced by balancing the number of investments in each group and spreading investments over each group. This is called balancing a portfolio. Insurance is available on some investments to protect against some risks.

Debt Reduction

This is a type of investment because when you reduce debt, you save the interest that you would normally pay on the loan. The investment return is equal to the interest that you save.

> *If you have a credit card with a balance of $2,000 and an interest rate of 18%, you will be paying $30 in interest every month. If you have $2,000 in cash and want to invest it, you could put it in the bank with an interest rate of 6% and earn $10 per month.* ***But*** *if you pay $2,000 off the credit card, you will save $30 per month in credit card interest. You will be $20 per month better than if the money is in the bank.*

> *Thinking on a larger scale, by paying off your housing loan, rather than investing your money, you will be increasing your wealth by the interest rate on your housing loan. Personal debt reduction is a great way to save money; however, watch the interest rates. Always repay the loan with the highest interest rate first.*

Loans taken out for the purpose of investment are treated differently; therefore, debt reduction may not be the best option—see Property below.

Cash Investments

Term deposits held at a bank, cash management funds or government bonds all provide income in the form of interest. There is no growth in the investment; it has the same dollar value at the end of the term as it had at the beginning of the term. The value will go down by the rate of inflation. The investment is usually for a fixed term, and the interest can be added to the original investment to compound the benefit—or be paid at the end of the term. Cash investments are very safe, and the risk level is low. You can often withdraw your funds at any time, but you may incur a penalty fee for early termination. Cash investments also provide a known amount of money and are popular with retirees who depend on the interest for regular income.

Cash Investments Summary

- ✓ Capital Protection—low risk.
- ✓ Term of investment—short term to long term, choice of investor.
- ✓ Returns versus Growth—returns only, no growth.
- ✓ Leverage—not applicable.
- ✓ Tax—payable on income—no capital gain.
- ✓ Inflation—reduces the value of the investment but should be offset by the interest earned.

Shares

As businesses grow, they need to raise money to expand. Companies do this by selling shares. Shares can offer growth as the company, through its operation, becomes worth more. However, companies are also vulnerable to losses if they perform poorly.

With the development of the Internet and flexible share trading programs, more and more people are buying shares in other companies.

There are 2 common investors in the share market—short-term traders and long-term income holders. If you have time, availability at critical market changes, and the desire to bargain and take risks, share trading may suit you. It involves buying shares at one price and selling them for a profit, usually in a short-term turn around. This sounds easy; however, shares are volatile and can go up and down quickly without notice. This type of investing requires constant monitoring to be successful.

Long-term share investors buy and hold shares. Company profits are partially paid to the owner of the shares in the form of a dividend. This is comparable to interest paid to investors from a cash investment. They can also benefit from long-term capital growth, if they have chosen good quality shares.

If you like the idea of investing in the share market, concentrate on blue chip (good quality) companies to produce a regular income. If you invest speculatively with unknown companies, be prepared to lose your money. Look for companies that are winning in their industry and have sound business plans and good leaders.

Shareholders have no control over the price of shares in the market. Invest in companies whose business you understand and have regular, solid dividend payment plans.

Diversity in the share market can achieve some stability since one industry may climb when another falls. Consider reinvesting dividend payments to grow your investment.

Share Summary

- ✓ Capital Protection—can be high risk.
- ✓ Term of investment—trading can be very short (hours) but can be years for long-term holders.
- ✓ Returns versus Growth—dividend income is often higher than bank interest. Growth is very volatile and is influenced by world markets and local trends.
- ✓ Leverage—it is possible to borrow to buy more shares; however, this is a high-risk strategy.
- ✓ Tax—income tax is payable on dividend income, and capital gains tax is applicable when shares are sold at a profit.

Capital losses can only be offset against capital gains and not against other forms of income.

- ✓ Inflation—not a critical factor.

Helen's Tip:

Run the numbers before investing in <u>anything.</u>

Investing

> *There are a number of other types of investments created around the share market—from margin lending to equity portfolios. Most are subject to the same share market fluctuations, but they work in slightly different ways. Understand all the terms and conditions before you invest your money—and use reputable investing firms.*

Property

Owning property is not a get-rich-quick scheme. Properties tend to go up, stabilise, and not move. They may go down and then go up again. This is called the property cycle. You need to be in the market for at least one full property cycle, which can be ten years or more.

Consider the following before you purchase an investment property:

- ✓ Appoint a property manager to remove you from the stress of regular issues.

> *Defence Housing Australia offers guaranteed rent for the contracted period and takes care of all maintenance. (see webpage reference).*

- ✓ Ongoing cost of property ownership, such as insurance, rates, maintenance, and management and body corporate fees.
- ✓ Tenants—when choosing a property, consider one that will appeal to a tenant. Think about the sort of tenant you would like (family, students, groups, with or without pets.)

- ✓ Choose a well-presented property. Poorly presented homes tend to be poorly cared for by the tenants. Consider if you would you live there?
- ✓ Maintenance—what needs to be done and who is able to complete the task? Use washable paints and hard flooring to reduce damage.
- ✓ Location—properties within 9 kilometres of the central business district (CBD) usually rent well and receive higher rental income.
- ✓ Don't restrict yourself to areas you live in now.
- ✓ Look for growth and return—balance, depending on your current cash situation, stage in life and tax position.
- ✓ Negative gearing. When expenses are more than income, it causes a net loss on the tax return. It enables the investor to take advantage of capital growth in the future—and reduced tax in the current years. Often it does not relate to negative cash flow since depreciation can be claimed as an expense for tax purposes, but it does not mean a cash outlay from the rents received.

Buying a House with Cash Deposit and a Bank Loan.

Cost of House	$500,000 (asset)
Bank Loan	$400,000 (liability)
Deposit you put in	$100,000 (equity)
At this point, your worth is	$100,000.

Investing

If, over a year, the value of your house goes up by 10% to $550,000 and you repay 5% of the principal ($20,000) plus interest (if the interest rate is 7% on the bank loan of $400,000, interest would be $28,000 per year plus principal payments of $20,000 gives a total of $48,000 for the year), your equity would change as follows:

Value of House	$550,000
Bank Loan	$380,000
Equity	$170,000

Your worth is now $170,000 an increase of $70,000.

If you leave the deposit funds in the bank for 1 year and do not buy the house, after one year your bank account would look like this:

Opening balance	$100,000
Plus amounts not paid on loan	$48,000
Plus interest at 3%	$3,000
Equity	$151,000

Your worth is now $151,000, an increase of $51,000.

In this example the person who bought a house would have more equity or be worth more than the person who left the money in the bank.

Chapter 25

Property Summary

- ✓ Capital Protection—lower risk level as the investor has a real asset—*bricks and mortar*.
- ✓ Term of investment—long-term. Buying and selling houses is not really a practicable exercise, due to the high cost of each transaction—sales commission, taxes etc.
- ✓ Returns versus Growth—property can have both depending on the location of each house.
- ✓ Tax—tax will be payable on the net income from the property. It is important to understand what expenses are considered tax deductable. Improvements are not and should be depreciated. Capital gains tax is also applicable when you sell a property.
- ✓ Inflation—property is one factor in the calculation of inflation, and it usually keeps pace with inflation. This means that, as a cup of coffee increases, so does the house value—and the rent and expenses.
- ✓ Leverage—it is feasible and common to borrow against one house to purchase another house using the property as security by the bank. This way one investor can own many properties—all with loans attached. When the market increases, the investor's profit increases on the original investment—and on the borrowed funds.

The amount of borrowed funds does not increase.

The following table shows the effect on your equity if you buy one house and if you buy 2 houses. The cost of each house is $400,000 and the capital you have is $100,000. You will borrow the remaining funds. In this example, I have used a market increase of 5% per year over 3 years. As a comparison, I have included a cash term deposit with the same return of 5% per year.

Investing

	Buy one house	Buy 2 house	Cash Term Deposit
Cost	$400,000	$800,000	$100,000
Borrowings	$300,000	$700,000	0
Cash invested at start	$100,000	$100,000	$100,000
Value of houses after 1 year,	$420,000	$840,000	$105,000
Equity after 1 year	$120,000	$140,000	$105,000
Value of houses after 2 years	$441,000	$882,000	$110,250
Equity after 2 years	$141,000	$182,000	$110,250
Value of houses after 3 years	$463,050	$926,100	$115,762
Equity after 3 years	$163,050	$226,100	$115,762

Both of the property examples are using leveraged (borrowed) funds. At face value, buying 2 houses produces significant more wealth—and you have successfully *leveraged* your money to produce a higher gain. However, the property value may go down instead of up. There is a cost involved in borrowing the funds. There is also no maintenance or running costs in the above table.

It is a common practice not to reduce the loan for an investment since the interest is fully tax deductable. Excess funds can be used to reduce personal (non-tax-deductable) debt rather than investment debt. This practice is not recommended after retirement.

The greater the leveraging, the higher the returns. Higher return will carry a higher risk.

Other Types of Investments

Superannuation—tax incentives mean that a term deposit in a superannuation fund pays less tax than a normal individual. Superannuation funds are locked away until retirement and are subject to government regulations (*see chapter 27 for more information*).

Unusual investments

The following are good investments if the original quality is there. They can produce an income when sold value (growth), but they do not usually produce a regular income.

- Wine
- Artwork
- Precious Stones
- Jewellery
- Antique Furniture
- Collectables
- Gold

Where are you now?

Plan for the future

ALWAYS RUN THE NUMBERS

Chapter 26

Retirement

Stopping Full-Time Employment

Wealth—Freedom—Security

When to Retire?

For most people, retirement is when they stop full-time work. Type of employment, age, health, family, and financial status all play a role in determining the right time to retire. Your life goals and daily achievement plans should also play a part.

In retirement you have more time, but often less money.

Having sufficient money to complete your goals can make the difference between a happy retirement and a stressful one.

Plan your Retirement

Planning for your retirement during your working life, will ensure that there is sufficient money to stop work, live comfortably, and enjoy your plans with financial security.

> *Your **bucket list** will determine the amount of money you need. If you want to travel the world in first class, you will obviously need more funds than someone who is happy to sit by a beach and read a book. Start writing your bucket list now and keep it up to date.*

For some, retirement becomes a nightmare. Having sufficient savings, pension eligibility, superannuation, government benefits, investments, insurance, and taxes are some of the many issues to deal with when people get to a specific age—and there is no going back. There is a maze of new conditions and rules about when you can and can't do things, but there is a whole new breed of financial advisors to help you with complicated money issues.

It is important to protect your wealth and maximise your spending dollar.

The secret is planning. Really think about what you want to achieve in your retirement—daily, monthly, and yearly. What is going to keep you occupied and happy?

Helen's Tip:
Start thinking about retirement early.

Let us divide retirement into 3 categories. They affect each other and need to be considered as a package.

Money (of which you generally have less).

- Superannuation.

- Pensions.
- Taxes, Rebates, and Tax Offsets.
- Change in Income and Expenses.

Time (of which you generally have more).
- Traveling.
- Gardening.
- Community Work.
- Family Activities.
- Hobbies.

Emotional needs (which change when you stop working).
- Work-colleague Relationships.
- Partner-relationship Needs.
- Life Challenges.
- Male/Female Needs.

Money

Planning and saving when you are younger will add significant benefits to the amount of money you have in your retirement because of the compounding nature of savings.

> *If you deposit $1,000 into a bank account with an interest rate of 5%, leave it and the interest there for 30 years, it will be worth $4,321.94—more than 4 times the original deposit. If you only deposit this amount for only 5 years, it will be worth $1,276.28.*

> The sooner you start to save, the more money you will have.

The money does not need to be in cash; it can be investments, houses, or shares.

How much money do you need?

To understand your future needs, calculate your money needs in today's terms. If the cost of living increases, the earning power of your retirement investments will too.

Step 1—Current Status

Start with today's figures.

- What is your current annual income from wages?
- What is your current income from investments?

Step 2—Retirement Annual Income

Adjust your annual income to determine your *retirement annual income*. Look at the following items and assess if they will increase or decrease your current income when you retire.

- House Repayments—reduce if you plan to own your home by retirement age.
- Car Running Expenses—may change if the number of cars in the family changes or the mileage you travel when you retire changes.
- Travel Budget—may increase or decrease.
- Other lifestyle items like entertainment and hobbies.

Chapter 26

Step 3—Goal Retirement Total Assets

Determine your *goal retirement total assets* required to produce the retirement annual income. Review the investments you prefer to hold and estimate how many you will need to own, in today's dollars, to produce the estimated retirement income.

Money Example:

Step 1—Current Status

Current annual income	$80,000
Preferred investment options are:	
Investment net income from property	$18,000
Investment income from cash	5.5%

Step 2—Retirement Annual Income

Current income	$80,000
Remove loan repayments	- 12,000
Reduce car expenses	- $4,000
Reduce household spending	- $5,000
Add an overseas trip each year	+ $9,000
= estimated retirement annual income	$68,000

Step 3—Goal Retirement Total Assets

Assuming your preferred investment options are property and cash. The ownership of 3 houses will provide an income of $54,000. This is a little short of your retirement annual income. It can be topped up with the income from a term deposit.

You need $68,000 - $54,000 = $14,000.
To earn $14,000, you will need $254,550 in cash invested with an interest rate of 5.5%. (14,000 divided by 5.5 x 100)

Retirement

The Goal Retirement Total Assets are:

> Own 3 investment houses and have
> $254,550 cash in the bank.

These assets will produce:

Investment houses - 3 x $18,000 = $54,000
Cash - $254,550 x 5.5% interest = $14,000
Total in today's dollars = $68,000

As the cost of living goes up, the income earned by your assets goes up. Try not to focus on the amount in the early days; understanding the goal is the first step to financial independence. It is easy to adjust the goal retirement income as your circumstances change.

> *If you travel a lot during your working life, your retirement annual income can be reduced by the travel expense amount. This would mean your assets can be reduced to the income from 3 properties, and no cash.*

Helen's Tip:

Review your goal retirement assets every 5 years.

Achieving your goals is the second half of financial security in retirement. Once you know the goalposts, you can start planning how to kick the goal. The sooner you identify how wide the goalposts are, the longer you have to get it right.

Superannuation (*see Chapter 27 for more details*)

Superannuation is funds invested by your employer on your behalf. The funds are your money and should be considered part of your retirement assets. When you retire, your superannuation will change from a savings asset to an income-providing asset.

Government Pensions

If you have reached retirement age, the government pension ensures you will have a basic income. However, restrictions of income, assets, and age make many people ineligible for government pensions. In fact, compulsory superannuation contributions are designed to replace the pension in the future for many people. Since the rules are subject to government regulation, they sometimes change. (*See the government website for the current rules. www.centrelink.gov.au)*

When you reach the qualifying age (*governed by Centre-link*), your eligibility will be assessed. Currently the qualifying age is being changed each year until 1 July 2023, when it will be 67. Consider this age with your other retirement plans.

Tax, Rebates, and Concessions

In essence, the tax rules do not change once you retire. However, the tax applied to superannuation funds and certain types of investments do change. The tax on superannuation funds that have been accessed also varies depending on if you removed the full amount and reinvested it, or if you left money in your superannuation fund and drew a regular income.

Retirement

Once you retire, you can often live on less income. If you fall into a lower taxable income bracket, less annual tax is payable. Retirees can receive many rebates and concessions, including discounted travel, utilities, and rent assistance. Many companies offer retirees cheaper options.

> *Always,* **Run the Numbers** *before you make the big decisions regarding your money and retirement. The decisions you make now, could affect the rest of your life.*

Retirement Investments

Some investments are specifically designed for retirees.

Annuities are investments where both the capital and the interest are paid tax-free for investors over 60 who have invested with superannuation money.

Allocated pensions can only be purchased from superannuation funds and provide tax-free income if you are 60 years or older.

Term deposits can be created with money withdrawn from a superannuation fund, but they are subject to tax.

Investments that have accumulated outside of superannuation guidelines are generally taxed at the regular rates for individuals.

Be particularly cautious of get-rich-quick schemes, often targeted at retirees. You need to protect your investments carefully since they are difficult to replace.

Chapter 26

Saving Tips for Retirees

- ✓ At age 60, you can apply for a Seniors Card that entitles you to discounts on goods and services, including public transport, hospitality, and entertainment.
- ✓ Some people are also entitled to a concession card, which means they pay less for bills, including utilities and car registration.
- ✓ Many clubs and small businesses offer concessional rates for seniors. Always ask.

Time

Retirement can present you with some of the best times of your life—or it can be a time waster. Review Chapter 4 on Time Management to ensure you are happy with your future life plans. Time is similar to money and should be budgeted, planned, and assessed on a regular basis to ensure you stay on track and achieve your goals.

> *Sitting at home waiting for the big lotto win is not going to get you to your favourite holiday destination!*
>
> *Going on the cheap camping trip to Africa is only going to make those aches worse!*

Think things through and establish what is most important to you—even if they are silly little things.

> Do what *you* want and not what others want you to do or think you should do.

Divide your retirement up into 5 years phases. Set goals in each of the following groups to create a balanced lifestyle:

- ➢ Health and Physical.
- ➢ Household—includes gardening and maintenance.
- ➢ Emotional and Spiritual Well-being.
- ➢ Money.
- ➢ Relationships.
- ➢ Recreational Activities—includes hobbies and further education.

Emotional Needs

One of the biggest changes in life is retirement, and it can often affect people in different ways. Being prepared for the change will help ease the situation for you and those around you.

Understand what you will be able to achieve as you age, and how you will react to the new challenges in your life. Watch other people to assess their ages and capabilities. Although nobody is the same, you can get an idea of what you will be capable of in the future.

Consider how your day-to-day life will change and how you will react to the changes.

- ➢ How will you and your partner deal with not going to work?
- ➢ Will you be lonely?
- ➢ How will the 2 of you handle being in each other's company all the time?
- ➢ Be aware that males and females have different needs.
- ➢ What new challenges will there be in your life? Is it enough? Too much?
- ➢ What activities will keep you busy, stimulated, and active?
- ➢ How will you deal with health issues and restrictions?
- ➢ How will you deal with the death of your partner?

Take the time to make the best
of your retirement years.

Chapter 27

Superannuation

Savings that Cannot Be Touched Until a Certain Age

Superannuation is designed to provide money to fund members during retirement. The fund is operated in the best interest of the members and in accordance with various laws.

Superannuation contributions commence when you start work; your employer contributes a percentage of your earnings to your nominated superannuation fund on your behalf. You can also build your superannuation with your own contributions.

The fund invests contributions to earn money, which compound (*add to*) each year until retirement.

Superannuation has certain advantages.

- ✓ It is generally the most tax-effective way to save for retirement since funds are taxed at a lower rate than individuals are taxed.
- ✓ Earnings compound to increase your investment.

Superannuation

There are 2 disadvantages to superannuation savings.

> ➢ The money is not available until retirement age.
> ➢ The funds are subject to government regulation.

It is important to keep up to date with your superannuation policy. Keep track of regulation changes to ensure your savings are looked after properly.

There are so many variables to consider. It is important that you do your homework and seek professional advice.

Superannuation is real money—and it belongs to you. A little understanding now could mean a lot of extra money in the future. Do not think superannuation is only for old people!

> *The government co-contribution scheme is where they match employee contributions (under certain guidelines). This is a wonderful scheme to get extra money into your superannuation fund and applies to all ages (some limits apply).*

Contributions

Superannuation Guarantee Contribution (SGC) started 1 July 1992 and requires all employers to contribute money on behalf of its employees to a registered superannuation fund.

Choice of superannuation funds came into place in 2005. Since then, employees can nominate the superannuation fund their contribution is sent to. This reduces the number of superannuation funds each employee accumulates as they work for different employers. The only exception is if you are covered by a workplace agreement or an award that specifies a superannuation fund to be used by the employer.

Contributions are paid monthly or quarterly by the employer to a registered superannuation fund. The current rate is 9% of ordinary earnings for employees between 18 and 65 who earn more than $450 per month. This rate is being increased incrementally each year to 12%, starting from 1 July 2013. The percentage is set by the government and is subject to change; it is wise to review current guidelines.

> *It is at the employer's discretion to pay superannuation contributions for people under 18 and over 65 and those who earn less than $450 per month. They can also choose to pay a higher percentage.*

Additional superannuation contributions can be paid by the employee as deductions from their earnings or as an after-tax payment. Contributions are classified depending on how the tax has been calculated on the original earnings.

Non-concessional contributions are when no deduction has been claimed in your annual tax return. Concessional contributions are when a deduction is claimed on the employee's tax return. The superannuation fund does not pay any tax on contributions since tax has already been paid by the member.

Both concessional and non-concessional contributions have a maximum allowable limit (*superannuation contribution caps*) before extra tax has to be paid. Non-concessional contribution limits are 3 times the concessional contribution limit for each year due to taxes already paid.

Salary sacrifice contributions are when employees contribute pre-tax wages directly to their superannuation funds. This reduces the amount of income tax paid by the employee on their regular pay. Salary sacrifice contributions are considered a tax-effective method of saving; superannuation funds enjoy the lowest tax rates (*currently 15%*) in the system.

For self-employed people, superannuation contributions can generally be claimed as a deduction and reduces taxable income.

Funds

The better your superannuation fund performs, the more money it makes for you. Commonly an investment manager will be investing your superannuation contributions in line with government approved investments. All investments are subject to market change and can go up or down. Superannuation funds are generally looking for long-term performance in investments.

The most common type of fund is called an *Accumulation Fund*. The amount of money you get when you retire (*your retirement benefit*) depends on how much you contribute and the earnings from investing your contributions. The fund divides its investment earnings and pays your share to your account. *If* the fund loses money, your share of the loss is deducted from your account. The fees you pay in these funds should be set out in the product disclosure statement and vary from fund to fund.

The second type of fund is the *Defined Benefit Fund*. In these funds, the money you receive when you retire usually depends on how long you have worked for your employer and how much money you are earning when you retire.

If you have multiple superannuation funds, it is worthwhile to consolidate them into one fund to avoid paying multiple management fees. Most superannuation funds are happy to move money from another fund into their funds; it is only a matter of asking them to arrange the paperwork.

Self-managed Superannuation Funds (SMSF)

Self-managed superannuation funds allow people to control their own superannuation investments, according to the written investment strategy and the government regulations governing all superannuation funds, such as annual reporting to the Australian Taxation Office and compliance audits.

The difference between a self-managed superannuation fund and an industry or managed superannuation fund is that the members run it for their own benefit and are the trustees of the fund. The superannuation fund must be separate from personal and business affairs.

Contributions can be made to self-managed superannuation funds just as they can for other superannuation funds; however, most assets cannot be transferred. Superannuation funds generally are restricted in borrowing money.

Plan Your Investments

Most superannuation funds let you choose between different investment strategies and options (*property, shares—local, foreign, etc.*). If you do not make a choice, your money will be invested in the default superannuation strategy. Different strategies involve different levels of risk and return—and affects how your superannuation grows.

Keeping Track of Your Superannuation

Superannuation funds are required to provide each member with an annual statement, detailing contributions made by employers and members, profits or losses made by the superannuation fund, and other transactions on the account, such as fees and charges.

Employers are also required to inform employees of the contributions made on their behalf. It should be a simple task to match the 2 reports each year to ensure the amount your employer has paid was received by your superannuation fund and has been recognised appropriately.

There are many superannuation fund managers ready to invest your money. It is important to ensure your investments are with trustworthy companies you feel comfortable with. Industry superannuation funds are specifically designed to accept contributions from within specific industries and are dedicated superannuation companies.

Financial institutions and banks often have a superannuation branch that accepts contributions and invests according to financial criteria. There is more flexibility and investment choice structure within these superannuation funds than in industry superannuation funds.

Chapter 27

Accessing Your Funds on Retirement

When you reach your preservation age (a table showing these ages can be found on the ATO website) and retire or turn 65 (even if you haven't retired), you can access your superannuation. Superannuation funds can be paid as a lump sum or kept in the superannuation fund and paid in regular payments, much like a pension. The Government offers tax incentives for you to keep your money within the superannuation environment as a way of encouraging people to make their money last.

If you are a temporary resident working in Australia you can apply for your superannuation to be paid out when you permanently leave the country.

How tax applies to your superannuation benefit depends on your age and whether the superannuation comes from a taxed or untaxed source. It is also affected by whether the benefits are being paid as a lump sum or a pension. Taxation rules are subject to government change. It is critical to understand the tax implications of your superannuation *before* retirement. To work out how your payout will be taxed, you need to know:

> ➤ The part of your payout that is taxable.
> ➤ Your age when you receive the payout.
> ➤ How you receive the funds—a lump sum, a pension, or a combination of the 2.

From 1 July 2007, superannuation payouts are made up of a tax-free and a taxable component. The taxable component can be taxed (when the superannuation fund has paid tax on it) or untaxed (when no tax has been paid by the fund). The

Superannuation

superannuation fund will provide you with a payment summary that will show:

- ➢ The component of the benefit that is untaxed.
- ➢ The component of the benefit that is taxed.
- ➢ The tax withheld.
- ➢ Any tax offset you may be able to claim.

Once you have all the above information, it is possible to evaluate the most effective method of receiving your superannuation payments.

Superannuation can also be accessed by the estate upon the death of an individual.

More information about rates, thresholds, and minimum and maximum amounts can be found on the ATO web-site.

Chapter 28

World Economy

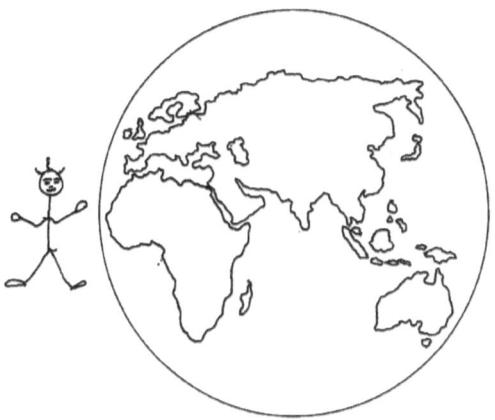

Ever since the turn of the century, the world has become a smaller place in which to live and work. People in the tiniest towns are now able to talk to people in the largest cities—anywhere in the world. Travel has become cheaper and easier to arrange for the everyday person and business incorporates travel as a normal part of life. The Internet is available via phones and computers, at home, at work, in the street, and on planes;—it is everywhere. Anyone can talk, transact, or simply find out information on anyone, anywhere, anytime.

So what does this have to do with me?

Different countries have very different lifestyles, cultures, beliefs, and traditions. These differences bring varied monetary ideas. As the world grows smaller, these differences can have an impact on our way of life. Of key importance are:

- Rates of Pay.
- Standards of Work.
- Distribution of Wealth.
- Value of Goods and Services.
- Quality of Products.
- Honesty of Trade and Corruption.

No longer can you sit in your home and be comfortable that the ways of different countries will not affect your life. Now, and in the future, your life is going to become more and more affected by what happens in other countries.

> *Consider the clothing industry. Much of the clothing we buy is manufactured in Asia by people who are paid a fraction of the standard wage in Australia. They are able to produce cheap clothes, which are favoured by the budget-conscious buyer. This affects clothing produced in Australia made by higher-paid workers. The Australian products cost more to produce and will be sold for more than clothes produced in Asia.*

In the past, the government protected Australian industries with tariffs, import duties, and taxes (similar systems are in place in most countries), but these practices are stopping and Australian products need to compete with global products without this assistance.

How does affect you?

As a consumer, you have choices about what you buy and where you buy it. In the past, your choices have been somewhat limited by the government protection schemes and by what was available in the shops. The Internet and reduction of government protection has changed this. You now have a global shopping centre offering many, many more options with varied prices and qualities.

What will you choose?
How will this choice affect different industries?

Consumer choices will change industry locally and internationally. If consumers stop buying at real shops and start buying on the Internet, the retail shops will close.

No consumers means no sales.
No sales means no profit.
No profit means no shops.

> We have seen this already in the petrol station industry. Some people remember when you went to buy petrol and a service attendant served you. This service no longer exists because a cheaper fuel price was offered if you served yourself. Over time, the pump operators could not afford to compete with the self-service operators—and now you can no longer find any fuel stations that offer service.

World Economy

Is this the way supermarkets and department stores will go? How will this affect the workforce? Will this mean there will be no more unskilled jobs available for teenagers or others who rely on unskilled work for income?

How you shop *does* affect industry

The Basics

- Supply and Demand.
- Interest Rates.
- Inflation.
- Employment and Unemployment.
- Government Debt.

Supply and Demand

The laws of supply and demand determine the price and availability of all products across the world. This basic rule of economics covers goods, services, money, and investments. Without demand, there would be no supply. However, without supply, there can be no demand since people do not know the product exists. The Internet has changed the supply side of this equation, and people's choices are changing the demand side of this equation.

Cost influences the consumer's choice in purchases. The cost of local product changes depending on supplier and marketing costs; however, the cost of overseas products is influenced by currency fluctuations as well. For this reason, everyone needs to have a basic understanding of international currency trade and how it affects the products they choose.

Chapter 28

The supply and demand for a country's currency can change from day to day, which affects the exchange rate between currencies. The more demand, the higher the value against another currency—and vice versa.

The value of each currency affects the ability of people overseas to buy local goods, services and money. It also affects the ability of locals to sell goods, services, and money to overseas customers. When the value of the local currency goes up, products in other currencies go up—and it becomes more expensive for the overseas customer to buy local goods. They may buy goods and services in their own country instead of looking overseas. Exports can fall at this point. On the other side of the coin, when overseas products cost less, imports usually rise.

A good indicator of prices and markets is the movement in house and new car prices and sales. In some countries, the price of a standard Big Mac is used as an economic indicator.

Supply and demand continues to pull the economy until balance is achieved. This balancing act occurs when a new product hits the market at a high price and drops to a lower price 6 months later.

Customers have the final say.

Interest Rates

Interest rates affect the amount of money investors borrow. If the interest rate is high in one country, the investors' money will earn more income in that country—and they will therefore choose to purchase currency from this country. This increases demand for that currency, which increases the value or the exchange rate of that currency. This occurs in countries with a floating currency and a central bank (Reserve Bank of Australia) to control inflation by varying the interest rates. The central bank controls the interest rate it applies to all other bank transactions. Independent banks set interest rates based on the central bank's interest rates, plus operating costs of the business. They are closely related but do not necessarily have to go up or down at the same time.

Inflation

Inflation is the difference in the amount that an identical basket of goods costs from one year to the next. It is calculated on a range of products to try to give an overall rate for the entire country. With high inflation, the cost of living increases, which can only be met if the income that people earn also goes up. When inflation is higher than wage increases people will stop buying some goods and services; this is called a *slowing of the economy*. Price increases will also slow as fewer products are sold and, in turn, inflation slows. At a low inflation rate (under 5%) *economies are stable*—although there is always movement in the market.

In slow-moving economies, governments borrow funds to invest in large scale projects to employ people. When people are employed, they earn money and they spend money. This *stimulates the economy*. Money is moved around more freely and this activity can encourage inflation. Demand becomes higher and business is able to increase prices, which *causes inflation*.

Chapter 28

Unemployment

The unemployment rate is calculated by the government, based on the number of people registered as unemployed over the number of people actually in work. High unemployment is not good for a country because these people do not have money to spend and depend on the government for benefits. They do not have money to contribute to the economy.

The government may try to reduce high unemployment by increasing government spending and employing people; however, this can increase government debt.

Government Debt

Government debt is the amount of money owed by a government. As with most loans, there is interest to be paid and this—plus the repayment of the debt—must come from government income. This is mostly derived from taxes. Just like individuals, if a government borrows too much money it can be difficult to repay the debt.

They can choose to increase earnings to cover debt payments by increasing rates and taxes; however, this is unpopular with voters.

The government can also choose to reduce spending, which tends to result in a loss of jobs and is also unpopular with voters.

Stable and consistent government monetary policies produce stable economies, but global forces can affect even the best plans.

The following picture shows how each area affects and is related to the other areas:

Growing Economy

Definition	Produces	Results

- Low unemployment
- More tax collected by Government

- Increases spending
- High product demand

- Products prices increase
- Interest rates increase
- High inflation rate

- Over spending
- Increased debt

Slowing Economy

- Jobs lost
- Reduced spending
- Increased debt payments

- Less tax collections

Economy stalls—can cause a recession
Government Stimulates Economy

- Increases Government spending
- Employs people

- Increases Government debt

- Lowers interest rates

- Less savings

Conclusion

Knowledge is power

Knowledge about money comes from understanding the jargon and applying your knowledge to products that you are personally comfortable with. It is not difficult, and anyone can learn the tricks of the trade.

Set Goals

All the information in the world is useless without knowing what you want. Understand that everyone has different needs, comfort zones, and goals that will send us down different paths in life.

All goals require a plan to achieve success.

Accept Change

One of life's certainties is change; the plans you make today will change tomorrow. At different stages in your life, research and obtain the knowledge you need to make informed decisions.

Money is not everything

Money is only a tool to make things happen in your life. Do not let it, or the people who work with it, control your life.

Be Happy and Enjoy life.

Helpful Websites

When researching any subject, be aware of the validity of the information. If in any doubt, always consult a government or legal site rather than a community site.

- ✓ www.ato.gov.au—the Australian Taxation Office
- ✓ www.ato.gov.au/superannuation—the Australian Taxation Office (Superannuation section)
- ✓ www.invest.dha.gov.au—Defence Housing Australia
- ✓ www.fairwork.gov.au
- ✓ www.centrelink.gov.au
- ✓ www.moneysmart.gov.au

State tax websites

- ✓ www.osr.nsw.gov.au
- ✓ www.osr.qld.gov.au
- ✓ www.sro.vic.gov.au
- ✓ www.osr.wa.gov.au
- ✓ www.revenuesa.sa.gov.au
- ✓ www.revenue.act.gov.au
- ✓ www.revenue.nt.gov.au
- ✓ www.sro.tas.gov.au

Sample Worksheets

The following worksheet guidelines have been included to help keep your money matters in order and easy to find. If you are using Excel, please go to the website and down-load the formatted sheets. If you are not using Excel, use the heading across the page add up the sheet each month, and check it against the total column.

The best practice is to update each sheet monthly. Some should be printed each month for record-keeping, and some are printed and kept in a see-through folder for reference.

- Balance Sheet
- Income and Expense Statement
- Budget
- Income and Expenses with Budget
- Insurance Summary Sheet
- Loan Schedule
- Run the Numbers
- Review Sheet

Sample Worksheets

Balance Sheet

For full details see

Chapter 14

This report shows where you are now and what you are worth.

Record:

Assets (things you own)
Liabilities (people you owe money to)

Calculate—Equity

Total each column.
Equity = Asset—Liabilities.

Balance Sheet

Date (a point in time)   January 2013

Assets Name	Amount	Liability Name	Amount
list the things you own		*list people you owe money to*	
Current Assets		**Current Liabilities**	
Example:		*Example:*	
Bank	$100.00	Credit card	$750.00
Total Current Assets	**$100.00**	**Total Liabilities**	**$750.00**
Fixed Assets		**Non Current Liabilities**	
Example:		*Example:*	
House	$200,000.00	Bank Loan	$150,000.00
Total Fixed Assets	**$200,000.00**	**Total Non Current Liabilities**	**$150,000.00**
Total of all Assets	**$200,100.00**	**Total of all Liabilities**	**$150,750.00**

Equity   **Total Assets less Total Liabilities**   **$49,350.00**

Sample Worksheets

Sample Worksheets

Income and Expense Statement

For full details see

Chapter 15

This report shows money earned and money spent—it shows the surplus or shortfall (deficit) with your money for every month and year to date.

Record:

The types of income you receive (wages, allowances, interest) and then total the amount for each month.

The types of expenses (rent, phone, car, food) and then total the amount for each month.

Calculate—Surplus or Shortfall

Total income for each month.
Total expenses for each month.

Surplus or Shortfall = total income - total expenses. A positive number is a surplus, and a negative number is a shortfall.

Sample Worksheets

Income and Expenditure Statement

Period of time   April 2013

Type of Income	Amount
list the money you have earned	
Example:	
Pay	$2,050.00
Total Income Earned	**$2,050.00**

Types of Expenses	
Example:	
Rent	$800.00
Phone	$75.52
Total Expenses	$875.52

Surplus $1,174.48

Note: if the Surplus figure is a negative you have spent more than you earned this month.

Sample Worksheets

Budget

For full details see

Chapter 16

Record:

Types of income and expenses.
Story or calculation of how you estimated a budget number.

Calculate—Budget

Estimate the total income and expenses for the year.
Total income - total expenses = budget surplus or shortfall.

Headings:

Type of income		Budget Amount	
or type of expense	Story	Month	Year

Use your budget to produce a cash flow statement.

Use the budget in the Income and Expenses budget analysis to monitor differences between what is actually received and spent to what was budgeted for.

Sample Worksheets

Budget
Period of time — 2013 Year

Type of Income list the money you have earned	Story *Describe how you calculated the amount*	Amount - Month	Amount - Year
Example: Pay	*500.00 per week*	*$2,000.00*	*$26,000.00*
Total Income Earned		**$2,000.00**	**$26,000.00**
Types of Expenses *Example:*			
Rent	*200.00 per week*	*$800.00*	*$10,400.00*
Phone	*50 per month*	*$50.00*	*$600.00*
Total Expenses		**$850.00**	**$11,000.00**
Surplus		**$1,150.00**	**$15,000.00**

note if this figures is a negative you have spent more than you earned this month rework the budget until a surplus occurs.

Sample Worksheets

Income and Expenses with Budget

For full details see

Chapter 16

Record:

Actual income and expense for the month
Budget income and expense for the month

Calculate—Differences

The difference between the budget and the actual income and expenses is calculated for each type of income and expense.

Difference = Budget - Actual.

Income—if the difference is negative you have received more than you budgeted for. If the difference is positive you have not received as much as you budgeted for.

Expense—if the difference is negative, you have spent more than you budgeted for. If the difference is positive, you have spent less than you budgeted for.

Income and Expenditure with Budget
Period of time January 2013

Type of Income	Actual Amount	Budget Amount	Variance Amount
list the money you have earned			
Example:			
Pay	$2,100.00	$2,000.00	-$100.00
Total Income Earned	**$2,100.00**	**$2,000.00**	**-$100.00**
Types of Expenses			
Example:			
Rent	$800.00	$800.00	$0.00
Phone	$45.72	$50.00	$4.28
Total Expenses	**$845.72**	**$850.00**	**$4.28**
Surplus	**$1,254.28**	**$1,150.00**	**-$104.28**

Note: if the Surplus figure is a negative you have spent more than you earned this month.
If the total of the variance column is a negative number, the actual amounts are better than the budget.

Sample Worksheets

Sample Worksheets

Insurance Summary Sheet

For full details see

Chapter 20

Record:

Information on all insurance policies you have.

Headings:

Record the following headings across the page and then list each item down the page, completing the details.

What is insured
Company name
Term or period—this will show when it needs to be paid
Amount paid
Date paid
Policy number
Special Clauses e.g. excess

Update each time a policy is renewed and compare it to last year.

Keep the previous year's information as a comparison.

December 2012

Insurance Company	Period	Amount	Date Paid	Policy Number	Special Clauses
JJ Insurance	1 Jan - 31 Dec	$300.00	12/22/2011	M12456	200 excess
JJ Insurance	1 Jan - 31 Dec	$150.00	12/22/2011	B456789	no excess

Sample Worksheets

Loan Schedule

For full details see

Chapter 9

Record:

Details on all loans you have.

Headings

Record the following headings across the page and then list each item down the page, completing the details.

List the highest interest rate at the top and the lowest at the bottom.

Type of Loan
Lender
Term
Total amount borrowed
Interest Rate
Loan ID or number
Date completed

The goal is to repay the loan with the highest interest rate first and save.

Loan Schedule
Last updated   December 2012

Type of Loan	Lender	Term	Amount Borrowed	Interest Rate	Loan ID or number	Date Completed
Example:						
Credit Card	Bank1		$2,155.00	22.50%	1234 5678 7891 0000	
House	Bank1	10 years	$5,000.00	7.50%	CB4455	May-18

Sample Worksheets

Run the numbers

For full details see

Chapter 6

Record:

Information on available options. This form can be used for reviewing loans, purchase contracts, assets or investment proposals.

Calculate—the best money option

Calculate the total to be paid initially and for the total period.

There are always other factors to consider, such as personal preference and emotional likes and dislikes. Knowing the cost gives you valuable information to help you make the best decisions.

Run the Numbers

Review Item		Example:	Telephone plan
Period (example = 3 years)	3		
	Option 1	Option 2	Option 3
Initial Costs			
Example:	Plan A	Buy phone outright	Plan B
Upfront purchase	$0.00	$800.00	$0.00
Fees	$15.00	$0.00	$35.00
Total Initial Costs	**$15.00**	**$800.00**	**$35.00**
Ongoing Costs			
Example:			
Administration	$5.00	$0.00	$5.00
Monthly Charge	$50.00	$0.00	$57.00
Total Ongoing Costs	**$55.00**	**$0.00**	**$62.00**
Ongoing charges for period	$165.00	$0.00	$186.00
Total Cost	**$180.00**	**$800.00**	**$221.00**

Now you know the true cost of the phone, this information can help you make the best decision.

Sample Worksheets

Review Sheet

For full details see

Chapter 19

Check sheet to ensure all documents are reviewed in the required timeframe. The due column requires the date for the next review and can be crossed out when completed.

The company columns are used for the names of the companies you used for the review. Company 1 will be the current company, and the next columns are for comparing other companies when the review date falls due.

Full details should be kept with the contract documents.

Sample Worksheets

Review Sheet

Contract	Due Date for Review	Company 1	Company 2	Company 3
Loans				
Example:				
Home	2020	Bank1		
Car	2015	Bank1		
Policies				
Example:				
Health Insurance	December	Health co		
Home Insurance	December	AAA		
Car Insurance	March	JJ Insurance		
Other				
Example:				
Telephone Contract	December	TelcoZ		
Electricity	December	ELC		
Water	December	ELW		

www.ingramcontent.com/pod-product-compliance
Lightning Source LLC
Chambersburg PA
CBHW031826170526
45157CB00001B/205